Gp86 01515

METACAPITALISM

. . . and the Rocket's Red Glare

*A Revolutionary Primer for the
Social, Economic, and Political
Rebirth of America*

R. Lee Zimmerman

UXOR PRESS • NEW YORK

Published by Uxor Press
New York, New York

Printed in the United States of America
1 2 3 4 5 6 7 8 9

Library of Congress Cataloging in Publication Data

Zimmerman, Robert L., 1940-
    Metacapitalism.

    Includes Index

ISBN 0-932555-00-4

DEDICATION

Metacapitalism is dedicated to the thousands, perhaps tens of thousands, of pamphleteers whose efforts
helped set in motion the First American Revolution. It is
further dedicated to three daughters, Linda, Deborah,
and Emily whose love was deeply inspirational.

Two roads diverged in a wood, and I—
I took the one less traveled by,
And that has made all the difference.
. . . . from "The Road Not Taken"

—Robert Frost

"The proliferation of means and the confusion of ends seems to characterize our age."

—Albert Einstein

ACKNOWLEDGEMENTS

Publication of **Metacapitalism** was greatly aided by the editorial and intellectual efforts of Gwyneth Lewis, who is now at Oxford University. Her labors were periodically supplemented by those of Patricia Schaeffer, Allison Lee, and Viji Seshardi. Elizabeth Levine prepared the bibliography. Special thanks to Stanley Seitel.

CONTENTS

CONTENTS

III

The Nature of American Capitalism: Why it is Uncertain

IV

Metacapitalism's Social, Economic, and Political Program for a Second American Revolution

CONTENTS

PREFACE

America's mission to sustain freedom against the encroachments of totalitarian communist imperialism has led to enormous expenditures for military equipment and personnel: expenditures which now consume six percent of our annual Gross National Product, or approximately $286 billion in 1986. Almost completely eclipsed by the magnitude and complexity of these expenditures for military preparedness are other vital aspects of achieving a strong national and international posture. America must reverse the course of the now dominant political and social ideologies which are shrinking our birthright freedoms; American democracy and capitalism must continue to evolve at an even faster pace than in the past and along humanitarian lines, rather than continuing to retrogress into a divided society ruled by a tiny minority of self-glorified, elitist, economic monopolists and their army of panderers. America must also vastly accelerate the pace of its domestic economic development by adopting national economic policies and strategies that reverse the debilitating efforts of the monopolists toward greater and greater economic concentration. Economic monopolism impedes economic development and the spread of economic prosperity: the current alliance of monopolists and government has made a mockery of our so-called free market economy and produced an insidious form of anti-competitive socialism entirely dominated by that same alliance. America must strengthen its relationships with freedom-loving nations throughout the world by pursuing non-exploitive free trade policies, exporting our technological achievements, providing technical assistance, and extending our traditional treaty obligations. Lastly, America must greatly intensify its assistance, particularly economic assistance, to developing and under-developed nations, including those struggling under communist rule; currently we allot less than two-tenths of one percent of GNP to providing economic assistance to imperiled or struggling nations.

Metacapitalism is a revolutionary primer for the social, economic, and political rebirth of America. It takes the ailing American Dream and turns it into a vision of a just and humane society. It professes the conviction that a stagnant and decaying America can once again achieve its ideals of expanding freedoms and equal opportunity for all men and women. *Metacapitalism* raises difficult questions about the American economy and society, and then proposes daring but humanitarian solutions to them.

At the turn of the twentieth century, and for twenty years following World War II, America seemed poised for greatness. Then uncertainty captured both capitalism and democracy. The initiative which was once the hallmark of the American spirit has now passed to other nations. In the economic competition with the Soviet Union, it is no longer clear that America will emerge victorious. Our political system has become cumbersome and corrupt, pandering to powerful special interest groups rather than serving the general interests of the American people. Our economic system is riddled with myths and insufficiencies. Social injustice and economic monopolism are rife and disgrace the spirit of our revolutionary Constitution.

Metacapitalism formulates the equivalent of a new Bill of Rights which eliminates those anachronistic inconsistencies which prevent America from realizing its declared ideals. This Bill of Rights would supplement our revolutionary Bill of Rights with twelve legislative initiatives to transform America's uncertain capitalism into *Metacapitalism* and spread freedom and economic prosperity throughout the land.

1. **The Voting Powers Act** enfranchises Americans to vote directly on important national issues, rather than relying on the actions of their elected representatives.

2. **The Prosperity Revenue Act** establishes a flat ten percent income tax, eliminating all tax deductions for individuals and businesses while vastly increasing government revenue and eliminating the federal deficit.

3. **The Income Security Act** provides a minimum guaranteed income and dignified retirement for all Americans. It establishes payment of a National Productivity Dividend which will significantly reduce poverty, as well as the need for welfare, unemployment benefits and Social Security.

4. **The Political Reform Act** seeks to streamline our bloated government by abolishing the House of Representatives, restructuring the Senate and the Supreme Court, and changing the duration of senators' and the President's terms in office.

5. **The National Education Act** will guarantee a higher education freed from financial obstacles to every qualified America.

6. **The National Medical Care Act** releases Americans from the uncertain burden of medical payments and reduces the economic stranglehold of the medical industry.

7. **The Economic Planning Act** imparts to the federal government responsibility for planning and managing the macroeconomy in a way that does not intrude on specific industries and businesses.

8. **The National Capital Act** provides significant financing to small businesses and farms from the government's general revenue and by deflecting investment away from monopolies and purely speculative ventures.

9. **The Corporate Reform Act** outlaws economic monopolism by placing limits on the size and discretionary powers of businesses and financial institutions.

10. **The Financial Reform Act** places limits on the activities of the nation's banking system, outlaws purely speculative financial instruments and markets, and puts a cap of five percent on interest rates. It thus significantly reduces the risk of severe recession or depression.

11. **The Community Participation Act** provides a significant flow of continuing revenue to local communities to assist with local problems, to encourage citizen participation in community work, and reduce citizen alienation.

12. **The Judicial Reform Act** modifies legal procedures to place life above property considerations and reduce the litigiousness within society.

Metacapitalism, beyond capitalism, was conceived to widen the dangerously narrow social, economic, and political ideologies that now dominate our nation. Impelled by a newly impassioned American electorate, the ideas that fashion *Metacapitalism's* proposed legislative initiatives will modernize our government, recapitalize American businesses and farms, and, most importantly, re-enfranchise the vast majority of America's citizenry. All of this is possible in a decade, although it could take several generations.

But Americans have too long endured the frustration of living with illusions: illusions of freedom, illusions of equal rights, illusions of equal opportunity. Since the very founding of our republic, property and class relations have dominated social and political relations. The aristocracy that our Founding Fathers fought to overthrow in the First American Revolution has regrouped and changed its clothes, but its major objective, to enslave the many for the benefit of the few, is as operative today as it was at the height of feudal Europe. The kings and princes, the royalty of old, are now the economic monopolists, the old guard of entrenched, inherited wealth. It will take a Second American Revolution, a revolution of ideas, to wrest America from their vice-like grasp and return it to the American people, in the immortal words of Carl Sandburg's, "The People, Yes":

RLZ

METACAPITALISM

Part I

METACAPITALISM INTRODUCED

AN INTRODUCTION
TO *METACAPITALISM*

As the twenty-first century approaches, America and the Soviet Union are locked in a trenchant battle for ideological, military, and economic supremacy. Much is known about the ugly arms race. The war of ideologies has been well documented and disseminated, at least in the free world, but the interpretive analysis of this vast documentation seems decidedly lacking. The economic war or competition, however, has received very little notice, although it is deadly serious, at least as far as the Soviets are concerned. The economic war is fought along ideological lines, though as ideologies both American capitalism and Soviet communism are fraught with ambiguities and inconsistencies. Fought with economic principles that are at best inconclusive, with people who are not beholden to a particular ideology, and with a seemingly inexhaustible supply of material resources, the economic competition is backed with threat of a full-scale nuclear war. It is ironic that those who entertain the notion of such a modern day Armageddon are inspired on both sides by the worn-out policies and the intellectual debris of the eighteenth and nineteenth centuries. The myth of American democracy and its associated free market economy is a gigantic fraud, as is the myth of the omni-present Soviet. Such imprecise theoretical constructs are more than delusions. They are extremely dangerous. The on-going clash of nations and notions, capitalism and communism, democracy and tyranny, archaic and atavis-tic attitudes, jeopardizes daily the lives of billions of human beings.

At the same time, as long as there has been life on our planet it's quality has been extremely poor for most of the world's citizens. While a fortunate few indulge in excess, most of the world's population is consigned to conditions of incredible poverty. This dangerous situation demands a solution. To drag these problems on into the twenty-first century without a remedy would be a dis-grace. But what can be done? Serious-minded people of varying ideological persuasions differ greatly regarding the nature of the problems confronting us, the priorities involved, and possible solutions. Most of the thinkers who address these questions are intimidated to such an extent that their minds are numbed.

Metacapitalism is free of the institutional biases that plague many reformational approaches in the United States. If *Metacapitalism* makes use of historical dogma, it is only that dogma which posits freedom as society's greatest achievement. At first sight, this seems to pit *Metacapitalism* against Soviet communism. In reality, it would serve as a bridge between American capitalism and Soviet communism. *Metacapitalism* seeks to fashion a

Second American Revolution, a revolution to recreate America's institutional infrastructure, to demythologize American capitalism and the economic theorems upon which it rests, and to transform America's so-called democracy into a true democracy, a democracy of, by, and for the people.

Metacapitalism is American capitalism thought out from a humanitarian perspective. It is a healthy, vibrant capitalism, imbued with attainable social objectives and social programs that are fashioned to serve the general interests of all Americans, rather than special interests. **Metacapitalism** is American capitalism aggressively modernized to meet the manifold challenges that confront us, to rout the economic stagnation that has stolen the future from American workers, to triumph over growing Soviet economic competition, and to spread prosperity to all Americans so that our current system of incentives may be sustained while all but the most intransigent poverty is eliminated.

The core of **Metacapitalism** is contained in twelve pieces of proposed legislation dealing with a wide range of issues, such as a revision of our current system of federal taxation, the guarantee of higher education to all qualified students, the provision of income and retirement security to all Americans, and the introduction of a plan for national health care. Yet, while proposing very concrete methods for moving from uncertain capitalism to **Metacapitalism**, we welcome new social thought and debate over America's social, economic, and political future. **Metacapitalism's** first priority is to replace uncertain capitalism with the most solid alternative possible, so that we may all live better and safer lives.

America must change. Without change there is only stagnation and decay. We must modify radically many of our most cherished institutions. We must cast off the economic and political myths that retard our developing social, economic, and political systems. The vital interests of not only our citizens, but also of people the world over depends on America's ability and willingness to set a new course as we approach life in the twenty-first century. *Metacapitalism* presumes that the vast majority of Americans share a strong desire to participate in solving the many problems afflicting our society. It also assumes that the rigid few who act as the caretakers of the status quo will be the most ardent enemies of change. The neurotic conservative mentality, with its false concern for the past, has somehow beaten us into a stupor of fear and lethargy. This we must reverse immediately. We must accelerate the tempo of social, economic, and political experimentation in America. To refuse is to deny our birthright and to sink even deeper into a swamp of mediocrity and despair.

The complex interrelationships and transactions that make up our economy today defy description. It is on that highly complex system that we all depend for our daily survival. Our advanced industrial economy is as crucial to our survival as the soil and climate of our agrarian past. It is *Metacapitalism's* intention to restore vitality to our economy by proposing an end to economic monopolism and the residual aristocracy that are strangling our economy and prohibiting the spread of economic prosperity.

AN INTRODUCTION TO METACAPITALISM

The general interests of the American citizenry are best served by a rechannelling of our productive capacities away from the giant corporations and trusts and toward small businesses and farms. The American economy is in dire need of a major reorganization if we are to preserve and expand our cherished freedoms. Our current system of economic organization is leading us dangerously close to fascism and an intolerant government characterized by rigidity, belligerence, and racism. It is a nation's economic organization that determines the critical relationships between its citizens, government, and the means of production. These relations, in turn, determine the nature and number of divisions within the economic production system, controlling ultimately the quantity and quality of goods distributed and services produced.

Metacapitalism proposes that certain structural changes to our current system of economic organization will bring immediate benefits to all our citizenry, while also serving as a positive cynosure for the rest of the world. By making our supposed free market system into a reality again, and by prohibiting economic monopolism, we can soon expand production to a point where no one will be hungry or homeless. Individual initiative and productivity, now sapped by exploitative monopolism, will rapidly increase, as will our quality of life and economic security. To repeat, *Metacapitalism* is fundamentally American capitalism refashioned from a humanistic perspective. It draws upon the ideology and economic experience of the Nordic nations. It shares the humanitarian vision of Sweden, Norway, and Denmark, their expressed desire to place the welfare of their citizens beyond predatory commercial practices and mean-spirited political objectives. *Metacapitalism* declares that a nation is truly great only when it responds to the needs of its weakest members.

Even though the economic and social accomplishments of Scandinavia have been outstanding, we must not copy its methods. Whereas the Scandinavian nations are made up of essentially homogeneous populations, we are not. Americans manifest an independence of character that is as critical to our well-being as our technological and material resources. We draw great strength from diversity. Thus, *Metacapitalism* seeks to capitalize on our strengths by promoting modular reforms to our economic and political systems, rather than one overly complex and misunderstood sweeping reorganization. There is a side of the question even darker than the selfish motives of the guardians of the status quo. The high degree of self-interest that so distinguishes the American spirit is possibly the greatest impediment toward achieving a just society operating under capitalism and democracy. A self-interested citizenry, though absolutely essential to both capitalism and democracy, becomes self-defeating when, as now, the various bases of power respond to narrow special interests before the general interests of society. In view of the evident shortcomings of policies and programs aimed at benefitting narrow or minority interests, *Metacapitalism* will propose only that which is to the advantage of all Americans. Not one person will be excluded from participation in any of the programs proposed by *Metacapitalism.*

For instance, *Metacapitalism* introduces the idea of a Productivity Dividend, an entitlement that will provide income and retirement security for all adult Americans. Much of what is perceived as our rapacious self-interest emanates, in fact, from our economic insecurity, our fear of not being able to earn enough income. A National Productivity Dividend will reduce economic insecurity by guaranteeing all Americans sufficient income to cover necessities and provide for a dignified retirement freed from financial anxieties. The Productivity Dividend will reduce the economic insecurity of citizens; the amount of the entitlement will be set at a level high enough to free everyone from abject poverty. It will also put an end to such bureaucratic nightmares as the administration of welfare, unemployment insurance, and Social Security, which is insufficiently funded to assure a dignified retirement for elderly Americans. Finally the Productivity Dividend will consign to the archives of history the degrading experience of welfare assistance which has unfairly stigmatized the least fortunate among us.

Though born of revolutionary seed, *Metacapitalism* nevertheless encourages peaceful change—not utopian reductionism, but radical structural modifications to our existing social, economic, and political institutions. Uncertain capitalism, as it is currently practiced in America, is threatened by two dangers—one is external, the other, perhaps more insidiously, is internal. Externally, we are threatened by the Soviet communists; internally by the intransigence of our institutional infrastructure, our governmental bureaucracy, and an array of economic myths and traditions, all of which serve the interests of the status quo and breed an excessive timidity, apathy, and fear of experimentation in our citizens.

Americans must act now to regain their sense of national and community purpose. There are no preconditions of action other than the raised expectations of a re-energized citizenry. America will again be great only when we have:

1. Spread prosperity to all citizens.

2. Acknowledged our moral obligation and evidenced our unselfish desire to assist less fortunate nations.

3. Transferred political power to a participating citizenry that openly and regularly demands that its leaders pursue the path to a just society.

UNCERTAIN CAPITALISM: LIFE IN AMERICA YESTERDAY AND TODAY

Each day we learn more about the nature and extent of our nation's decline, the spreading economic insecurity, the rising rate of poverty, our waning commitment to equal rights and equal opportunity, the rising tide of crime, pollution, and social, economic, and political stagnation.

Each day we witness our failed leadership, uncaring, groping for answers without compass or compassion; sinking further into the swamp of mediocrity; voicing optimism while shunning responsibility as the nation continues its aimless drift into decline and our citizens grow more and more apathetic.

Once, America's standard of living was the highest in the world; now other nations lead the way. Before 1950 our health care system was the world's finest, with Americans enjoying the highest life expectancy and the lowest rate of infant mortality in the world. In the last twenty-five years, however, the cost of health care has soared well above the rate of inflation and has even contributed to it. Many who desperately need medical attention must forego it for lack of funds. More than thirty million Americans have insufficient resources to pay for proper medical attention. This does not include the tens of millions more who would be financially ruined if a member of their family were to suffer a long-term illness. In other counties those not covered by health protection programs are usually the rich, who are self-insured. In America those not covered are mostly the poor and the elderly.

In 1983 and 1984 we witnessed a whole new phenomenon in America during a period of long overdue economic prosperity. In the past a growing economy meant that the lion's share of any economic growth would find its way by means of higher wages to the majority of working Americans. But this is no longer the case. Today, the real wage of the American worker is stagnant or shrinking; an invidious condition that is the direct result of our archaic economic system and the actions of recalcitrant leaders who work to prevent its modernization. In 1985 the purchasing power of the American worker is no higher than it was in 1960, which means that we have seen more than twenty-five years of wage stagnation.

Have we reached the end of the road? Is stagnation the destiny of the majority of Americans? Is growth in income and quality of life mere history? An examination of the events of the last quarter-century would make it seem so. Our ultra-conservative leadership tells us that such is so. Tighten your belts, my fellow Americans, hard times are here to stay.

But, looking around, we find that not all is stagnating. There have been many changes. Unfortunately, in terms of social progress and economic justice, much of the change has been negative. There has been some progress in achieving equal rights for women and minorities, particularly the black minority. But for many, these equal rights are no more than words. Equal rights to what? An equal right to a dismal future is no great victory.

But even these small successes are repeatedly tested by the conservative guardians of the status quo. Today, an estimated twenty to thirty million Americans live at or very near the poverty level, and many millions more fear, with good reason, that they too will soon experience poverty. Meanwhile, the gap between the wealthy and the poor has widened significantly. Our leadership is quite effectively transforming the miseries of the poor into vastly increased wealth and income for the rich.

Today, many elderly Americans live in a dismal retirement and worry that their sole source of income, Social Security, is constantly threatened. Our leadership says they would not tamper with Social Security. No sooner were they re-elected than they immediately proceeded to tamper with it. In our cities an alarming number of people are living on the streets and in alleys. Millions of American citizens, including infants, young children, and those who fought to protect us from foreign treachery, are experiencing the horrors of hunger. Many are dying for lack of food, medical attention, and shelter. Each day several million children of school age go hungry. Meanwhile, our government deploys policies intended to restrict the quantity of food grown by farmers. These insidious policies work only in favor of the giant farming combines, leaving vast numbers of small farmers ruined, or on the verge of bankruptcy, and millions of our fellow citizens hungry.

LOOKING BACK:
FROM FRONTIER CAPITALISM TO
UNCERTAIN CAPITALISM

The first American settlers were severely tested as they struggled to sustain life in the American wilderness. The memory of their brave and lonely battle is still vivid, passed on from generation to generation. That history is of an era lasting from 1500 to the end of the Great Depression in 1933. It was an era dominated by the frontiersman, the rugged individualist, and, with the onset of the Industrial Revolution, the so-called "captains of industry." These 430 years represent the first phase of capitalism in America. Let us call it frontier capitalism.

Life in America under frontier capitalism was marked by the absence of an intrusive government. The federal government had not yet grown into a bureaucracy, and the tax rate was low. Citizens could reasonably expect to keep most of what they earned. There were very few governmental programs to assist the needy and citizens expected little of government. These four centuries of American life were far simpler than the five decades to

follow. With no recourse to government assistance programs, Americans who fell on hard times could turn only
to their immediate families and private charities. Though
many charitable organizations had sprung into existence,
serving needy people from all walks of life, there was
then, as now, a painful stigma attached to the acceptance
of charity, and many suffered rather than be seen to be on
the dole.

The massive human devastation brought about by
the Great Depression (1929-1941) forced a significant
change in American life, most particularly in the way
Americans viewed the role of the federal government. The
numerous private charities were inadequately funded to
handle the subsistence needs of a large percentage of the
population during that time of national crisis. Only the
federal government seemed remotely capable of taking
action to relieve the massive human suffering of the Great
Depression and bring to an end the national economic
stagnation and decline. But what action should be taken?
As is the case today, those in charge of government were
not really for the people. They distrusted them, erected
many barriers between the people and the government.
What is more, the leadership had no real experience of
designing or implementing national economic policies or
programs to stimulate the economy and bring the devastation to an end. The government, headed by President
Herbert Hoover, dragged its feet. Many thoughtful Americans were so incensed by the government's inaction that
they chose communism as an acceptable alternative to our
failing frontier capitalism.

But, after learning the true nature of Stalinism; the treachery, the human carnage, the supression of all freedoms, the Gulag horrors, the geopolitical menace, most of those Americans who had supported the communist alternative disavowed it. Neither is socialism attractive. Recent French experimentation with state socialism appears to have been a failure. Furthermore, American socialists have never united strongly, nor have they ever attracted more than a scant following. Something had to be done. That something brought to an end the era of frontier capitalism and ushered in what we term here the era of uncertain capitalism.

With the election of Franklin D. Roosevelt in 1932, the federal government began to take an active, if awkward, role in the administration of national economic affairs. President Roosevelt's foremost priority upon assuming office was to put an end to the Great Depression by using government spending to stimulate the economy (thus creating much-needed employment) and by initiating government programs to assist the needy. Federal spending to stimulate the economy, which came to be known as pump priming, was then a novel idea, attributed to the British Lord J. M. Keynes. Roosevelt's experiments with Keynesian economics produced dramatic and positive results. Before long the American economy was once again on track, and by 1946 economic prosperity began to spread across the entire nation.

This transformation from a government indifferent to economic matters to one which was involved in national economics was never completed. The end of the Great

Depression coincided with America's immersion in World War II. Our government's attention was deflected to assisting our allies in the West and thwarting the Japanese threat in the East.

Today, we are left in the midst of that incomplete transformation. We still dwell in the era of uncertain capitalism that began with the end of the Great Depression. The current conservative government would have us return to the era of frontier capitalism. It seeks to dismantle the middle classes in America and return us to the naked exploitation that characterized life in America under frontier capitalism. The conservative government in power today is the government of the ancient aristocracy, and its central mission is the transformation of all working-class Americans into urban serfs who would have less to sustain them in times of crisis than the serfs of old. They could at least use the land to grow food. Government policy is specifically directed at destroying small businesses and farms in favor of giant corporations, combines, and trusts. It aims to reduce drastically the ability of poor and middle income families to send their children to college. Government policies are increasing the number of Americans living in or near poverty, widening the gap between rich and poor. The nation's unions are being intimidated. The union of state and church is being sought. These mean-spirited policies are the worst danger that has ever beset American democracy, worse than the Great Depression (which was primarily the result of governmental bungling and speculative excesses), worse than World Wars I and II, the Korean, and Vietnam wars, (in none of which was America directly attacked).

The neurotic conservatives seek not only to degrade and defile the American experience by thrusting us back to an earlier and highly repugnant era, they also seek to begin dismantling the freedoms of our birthright. Nothing is as great an anathema to fascism and totalitarianism as an educated, participating citizenry. Let us not let the conservative reactionaries have their way. There are other, brighter, possibilities for life in America. One way is to move forward, not backward from uncertain capitalism to frontier capitalism, but on to **Metacapitalism.** Let the third phase of the development of capitalism and democracy in America be the very best. Let not the purveyors of economic enslavement have their way. Let us examine **Metacapitalism.**

METACAPITALISM:
AN ALTERNATIVE FOR AMERICA'S FUTURE

Life in America today, as in the past, is impelled by an instinct for survival, albeit survival of a very different sort. The development of our advanced industrial society, as nurtured by those powerful few who profit from it and control it, has isolated the vast majority of Americans from the traditional means of production. The frontier is located today in the metropolis. In these cities there is no land for farming or for the construction of ordinary shelter. There are no animals or crops to feed upon, no natural materials from which to fashion rudimentary clothing. To survive in today's cities, Americans are totally dependent on employment. Without a job and an income, life becomes miserable, almost intolerable, for most Americans. Being without a job in America means that each of our birthright freedoms is significantly diminished. The right to pray in the church of one's choice, to assemble, to speak, to publish—all of these and more are surely undermined by unemployment, economic insecurity, and hun-

20

ger. Those who seek to intimidate working-class Americans into accepting lower wages, lower self-esteem, and lower expectations for the future know full well the deep fear Americans have of unemployment, and even better how to exploit that fear to their own advantage.

A transition from uncertain capitalism today to **Metacapitalism** tomorrow will place every American beyond the twin terrors of poverty and unemployment. For we have learned from observing the hardships that permeate our land that freedom in America without a life-sustaining income is no freedom at all. Furthermore, the denial of income to individuals serves no useful purpose, unless you consider the depraved delight some few experience from observing the torture of poor souls as useful. The millions of homeless who scrounge for sustenance in the streets of our cities, the millions of single mothers who awaken each morning without enough food to feed their children, the millions of impoverished Americans who are too sick to work, the tens of millions who are unemployed, and the tens of millions more who live in dismal retirement because the Social Security they had depended on to support their retirement has turned out to be barely more than enough to sustain life, all of these millions of people—fully one-third of our population—are truly needy and furthermore, unnecessarily underutilized within the economy.

The denial of an income to citizens serves no useful purpose. In possession of an income, a citizen may become immediately productive as a consumer. In advanced industrial nations consumers enrich capitalists and not the other way around. It is an ugly myth that consumers and workers are beholden to capitalists for their livelihood. Without mass markets there can be no mass production, for who would purchase all that soap and coffee, the millions of automobiles, refrigerators, and so on? Thus, the minimum condition for human dignity—a subsistence income—is thoroughly consistent with the minimum condition necessary to an advanced industrial society functioning under capitalism and democracy, that is, an adequately funded mass market. To deny a citizen an income in America today is both antagonistic to the general interest and a social and moral disgrace.

Metacapitalism's proposed National Productivity Dividend will provide a subsistence income for all adult Americans as well as serving to stabilize our crinkum-crankum economy by transforming our entire citizenry into productive consumers. The bureaucracy that now attends to welfare, unemployment benefits, and Social Security will ultimately wither away, as will the insidious welfare mentality, the anguish over economic security, and the miserable retirement of the elderly. They will find that the Productivity Dividend is more than twice what they received under Social Security. The Productivity Dividend is a fundamental entitlement of all Americans, rich and poor alike. Economic security for all Americans will greatly expand every citizen's freedom and significantly reduce class antagonisms.

Metacapitalism's ambition to expand upon our existing freedoms by establishing a fundamental entitlement to a baseline income and retirement security is but one part of a package of revolutionary reforms designed to alter the basic structure of the American economy.

Related to the problem of income insecurity are the troublesome anomalies of income inequality and the accumulation of wealth. While totalitarian economic systems like Soviet communism are driven by an elitist dictatorship that co-opts individual choice, substituting dogma and authoritarianism for freedom, American capitalism is driven by the creative force of individual entrepreneurs and the will of the American citizenry to improve its economic condition. We pride ourselves on this exercise of individual will and encourage it by rewarding those who are most proficient and diligent with higher incomes and accumulated wealth. The great disparities in wealth which result from this competition means that the poor, manipulated by the wealthy, are forced to compete with the odds stacked heavily against them.

Without economic incentives for diligence and innovation, society becomes a dull place. Such an affliction already plagues the communist way of life; their leadership is hard-pressed to solve it. When left without the appropriate checks and balances, the very income incentives that motivate us beyond that effort required for mere survival may threaten the survival of others, as is the case in America today. **Metacapitalism's** National Productivity Dividend, tax on individual and corporate wealth, and prohibitions regarding the amount of an inheritance, all serve as remedial checks and balances.

Presently, however, it is hard to overstate the extreme concentration of wealth in America. Traditionally, wealth

23

is determined by subtracting monetary liabilities from monetary assets. The remainder is wealth. Calculated in this manner, it is estimated that seventy-five percent of the nation's wealth is held by less than twenty percent of the population. But when we think about wealth, what it does, how it is used, we are thinking about something vastly different from the set of assets minus liabilities. A person with a heavily mortgaged home can hardly be said to be wealthy when he or she is totally dependent upon a job to pay off the mortgage and put food in the cupboard. If that person becomes unemployed and cannot immediately find similar employment, then the loss of the home is at stake. Foreclosure is the moneylender's term for the judicial process that ensues. Real wealth is, therefore, not the sum of the value of personal possessions but that set of assets over and above possessions that are available for raising income, be that for current consumption or reinvestment. When wealth is measured in this manner it is likely that fewer than five percent of Americans own or control more than ninety-five percent of the nation's wealth.

Basically, there are two kinds of wealth in America: earned and unearned. Unearned wealth is entrenched wealth; its holders are a pitiful throwback to the sort of insidious aristocracy that Americans rejected at the time of the First American Revolution. Born to positions of privilege and influence, they often shelter themselves from the rigors of equal competition and aggressively, though in an underhand fashion, seek more and more economic and political power over those born in less fortunate circumstances. They who have not one whit of experience in the competitive arena and seek to undermine the efforts of those struggling to establish a foothold, turning the forces of economic monopolism and political corruption against them. Much of that which is negative within the context of American capitalism and American democracy is directly traceable to the manipulations of holders of unearned wealth as they struggle in vain to justify their existence.

America's wealth is a common to which every citizen is entitled by dint of his or her individual effort. To the successful competitors will fall a greater share than to the less prosperous, but only for a lifetime. Although the abolition of inheritance would be widely unpopular, even amongst those who have very little in the way of property to pass on to their heirs, *Metacapitalism* maintains that vast inheritance is a crime against society, a cruel deception practiced upon inheritors, an obstacle to the realization of equal rights and opportunity, and should thus be limited to far more modest sums than at present. *Metacapitalism's* Prosperity Revenue Act, which would replace the entire current system for individual and corporate taxation, would significantly expand the tax base while lowering tax rates by imposing a modest five percent annual tax on personal and corporate wealth, and taxing away untoward inheritances.

OUR CURRENT GOVERNMENT: REPRESENTATION WITHOUT REPRESENTATION

Given the vast resources at the disposal of our federal government and the overwhelming humanitarian bent of the majority of Americans, it defies understanding that our government's socioeconomic policies have been so consistently shortsighted and mediocre. In the 1960s, Presidents John F. Kennedy and Lyndon B. Johnson attempted to establish a sense of decency and responsibility in our nation's socioeconomic policies by targeting legislation addressed specifically to the needs of the economically deprived and oppressed. Yet when legislation is targeted for specific groups, particularly when the population of these groups has little political clout, sooner or later programs enacted to meet their needs will be cut from the federal budget by conservative politicians financed by powerful special interests.

There has never existed a political system capable of guaranteeing the long-term duration of any right or privilege, regardless of how universal or important to its citizenry. Yet a vigorous participating citizenry is the best guarantee we have. Now, however, as America stands in desperate need of a major ideological and structural overhaul, our citizenry has become apathetic. It is alienated from the electoral processes and disillusioned with their choices. A grand litany of corruption, deception, amateurism, and pure folly has taken its toll on the American electorate. To raise our citizenry from its slumbers will require a clear agenda setting forth an enlightened and constructive set of priorities for the future. To start, *Metacapitalism's* Voting Powers Act proposes changing the very nature of our democracy from a primarily representative system to one led by the direct vote of citizens on particular issues. Once the citizenry has expressed its choices, those we have elected to execute our laws will be legally bound to follow.

It is fundamental to the American political tradition to posit freedom before anything else. Without freedom there can be no meaningful prosperity or economic justice in this country.

1. Freedom as defined by a participating citizenry is vastly superior to any dictatorship, be it monarchic or totalitarian.

2. Freedom will flourish within a democracy only when the government places the interests of the weak and the general interest over and above special interests, no matter how powerful.

3. Freedom requires that the ownership of property is a fundamental right of citizens and that govern-

ment's role is to balance human with property rights as defined by the citizenry.

4. Freedom requires no more of government than its vigorous creation of an environment conducive to the evolution of a just society in accord with the wishes of the citizenry.

If there is an introductory summary of the aims of such a government it would be:

Let each citizen participate and delight in society according to his or her personal choices and successes. But let those choices be tempered and modified by our collective responsibility for ensuring that the vulnerable among us do not suffer from basic want or deprivation. Our nation is truly great only when its successes extend to all among us and to other nations less fortunate.

In order to move from uncertain capitalism to **Metacapitalism** our federal government must relinquish its role as ambassador for the well-financed special interests. It must assume the more appropriate role of initiator of social momentum and enlarger of individual and societal freedoms. It should become the active transfer agent for our National Productivity Dividend and begin to set meaningful national, social, and economic objectives that stabilize, invigorate, and give direction to private industry. **Metacapitalism** shares the ideals of our revolutionary past, but considers them insufficient for an advanced industrial economy.

Today, the choice is ours. We may continue along our present course, locked into the rigid structures that define our lives under uncertain capitalism. Or we may demand that our leadership move toward **Metacapitalism**. **Metacapitalism** is the voice of transformation, a voice uninfluenced by institutional bias. It is **Metacapitalism's** task to accelerate the tempo of social, economic, and political change in America so that all of our people may participate in prosperity.

Part II

**THE DUEL FOR DOMINANCE:
AMERICAN CAPITALISM VS.
SOVIET COMMUNISM**

CAPITALISM VS. COMMUNISM

Capitalism as Evolutionary, Communism as Retrogressive:
The Historical Roots of Capitalism and Communism

It is a fundamental premise of **Metacapitalism** that capitalism evolved naturally from feudalism and mercantilism, while communism, as practiced by the Soviet Union, is considered a retrogression, a manifestation of the master-slave society of the pre-feudal era. Capitalism represents an advancement of the human condition, while Soviet communism embodies only man's ugly past. The Soviet government is devoid of the hard won provisions that make America a truly democratic country; it is devoid of the checks and balances on the power of government that guarantee those liberties the free world now takes for granted. While it is true that America's current uncertain capitalism may still be far from perfect, Soviet communism offers no hope at all for the future of mankind.

In order to understand the development of capitalism and communism, it is helpful to trace their origins back to early man. As soon as man began to fashion tools, he set in motion the historical processes that have led to the structure of our current socioeconomic systems. Tools enabled man to defend himself from attack by larger animals, to evolve from hunted to hunter, to pursue larger quarry. With tools, man became more productive, developing from primitive scavenger to farmer and herd keeper, from a solitary being to a member of a tribe or clan. Man's early tools thus led directly to the formation of the earliest societies where blood relatives combined their individual efforts in joint labor, allocating certain functions to men, usually those requiring brute effort and physical risk, like hunting or protecting the tribe or clan from intruders, and others to women, children, and the elderly. Here lay the roots of all future societies and civilizations and the very first manifestations of the specialization of labor.

From **Metacapitalism's** perspective the transition from subsistence living to a lifestyle accustomed to surplus significantly advanced the development of social structures, economic, and political systems. Surplus food, clothing, tools, and utensils could be stored for future use or traded for other items. It is from the production, storage, and trading of early surplus that the notion of private property and community property evolved. The accumulation of surplus, first as clan property, and then as private property, gave rise to such concepts as rich and poor, debtor and creditor, mergers, commodity, inheritance, money, nepotism, economic security, and so forth. In short, the origins of twentieth century socioeconomic sys-

systems can be seen in man's prehistoric period when the clan and the tribe arose as a result of the first surplus.

The Evolution of the Clan: Competition and Militarism

For perhaps two million years a primitive competition existed among the innumerable clans that inhabited the earth. The clans that prospered hired members of the less fortunate clans as workers, or lent them goods which, if not repaid, led to the capture of the less prosperous clan and the enslavement of its members. This vast and extended prehistory was the breeding ground for many of the social distinctions that plague us today. As they vied for wealth, status, slaves, and for territory, the very nature and meaning of the clan began to shift from familial and protective to aggressive and militaristic. The solitary hunter of early prehistory, who roamed the plains and forests in search of food, was now a nomadic warrior consumed with greed and wanderlust.

The Roots of Feudalism

Towards the end of the fifth century A.D., Rome was conquered by an alliance of militaristic clans who divided the Roman lands among themselves. Most of the conquered territories were seized by the military leaders, the most powerful of whom appointed themselves kings.

These new kings, possessors of immense tracts of territory, deeded most their property to their janizaries and myrmidons for use during their lifetime. After their deaths these became family property that could be inherited.

This succession was certainly not the first manifestation of the idea of inheritance, but it did represent the spread of its practice and the formalization of the law of primogeniture. Here, as well, lay the roots of feudalism. Land tracts deeded by the new kings to less powerful but allied combatants were known as "fiefs" and their possessors, feudal lords, who in return for their king's largess pledged continued military allegiance and financial support. Local peasants, along with newly freed slaves, became serfs who worked their new lord's land and were held accountable to him.

Soon villages and towns, with assorted merchants and specialized craftsmen, began to flourish around the huge feudal estates. Because the implements of farming were still crude and the tools of the craftsmen more sophisticated, nonfarm labor productivity grew at a faster pace than farm labor, and the villagers and townspeople began to demand more and more from their lords in exchange for their products. Their demands intensified the friction between serf and lord and forced the lords to demand a greater and greater share of the serf's agricultural product. The use of money, though already common, increased greatly at this time, as luxurious imports stimulated foreign trade, while the consumer demands of the lords exacerbated the already heated situation between them and their serfs.

The feudal estates, worked by millions of serfs under conditions only slightly less onerous than outright slavery, were a microcosm of early capitalism in several important respects. It was here that the essential goal of production transformed from immediate consumption to exchange. The feudal lords began to view the agricultural output of their serfs and the craftworks of the townspeople primarily as objects of barter, enabling them to buy the luxurious imports being made available in increasing assortments and quantities by the merchant traders. Here, too, one recognizes that the greed of the lords caused the grievous exploitation of serf labor. The rancor that has divided labor and management throughout America's capitalistic history is a product of the contemptible labor practices of the frontier capitalists, a direct carry-over from the feudal era.

Yet the serfs had far more to grieve about than the gruesome exploitation of their labor. Technically "freed" slaves (unlike the local peasants who could establish households, accumulate property, and train as craftsmen), the serfs were bound to the land as agricultural workers, forced to live their lives without benefit of property of any kind other than squalid clothing and common eating utensils. Anything else a serf was found to possess was quickly confiscated by the lord. Although it was technically illegal for lords to murder serfs the practice was widespread, as was the perfectly legal practice of selling or trading them. Thus, the distinction between serfs and slaves is tenuous at best.

Slavery in America

Slavery arose simultaneously in many of the numerous clans that inhabited Egypt, India, and China from the fourth to the second millenia B.C., and probably in other lands even earlier. In Rome slavery peaked between 2 B.C. and 2 A.D. The rich Roman estate owners had veritable armies of slaves, sometimes numbering in the thousands. Roman slaves were savagely mistreated, used as beasts of burden, whipped, tortured, herded, fed, and housed in pens like cattle. They were fed just the minimum to sustain life and the slightest malfeasance could lead to death. The murder of a slave by his or her master was not considered a crime—a legal convention that persisted even in America until the Emancipation Proclamation of 1863.

Slavery is still pervasive in modern society and permeates the consciousness of the descendents of its victims. In the United States, for example, American blacks still suffer from lack of self-esteem, suffer continuing discrimination, unemployment, and poverty. The injustice of their plight promotes a sense of bitterness which, though justified, is, unfortunately, self-defeating. It is not only in America that the effects of slavery survive. Slavery exists on an even more subtle and insidious level throughout most of the rest of the world.

Soviet Communism: A New Form of Slavery

Within the borders of the Soviet Union and its captive satellites may be found the largest slave population in the history of the world. 400 million people are indentured to the state, more than in the entire history of slavery before communism. It is a unique form of slavery.

The slavemasters are remote; and instead of whips and chains they employ tanks and troops. This vast slave population, though further from starvation and the daily horrors suffered by pre-feudal, feudal, and American slaves, will experience a similarly dismal fate. Their masters show no inclination to cut the people loose from Soviet bondage. Indeed it is the Chinese, and not the Soviets who, by renouncing Marxist-Leninist dogma and moving toward structures of capitalism, are the first communists to indicate a desire to free their citizens.

Soviet Communism: A Brief Historical Account

Soviet communism was ushered into Russia in 1917 when the Bolsheviks, led by V. I. Lenin, seized power from the Tsar Nicholas II. Under the pretense of freeing Russia's exploited masses, the Bolsheviks wasted little time implanting the communist ideology originated by Karl Marx and Frederic Engels. On October 26, 1917, only one day after seizing power, the Bolsheviks installed the Council of People's Commissars as the supreme ruling body of Russia. That same day the nationalization of all Russian land was formally announced, though the actual event had taken place earlier that year when the Russian peasants overthrew their landlords.

The Bolshevik decree of land nationalization, though officially abolishing private land ownership, left the land in the hands of the peasantry, who were competent farmers, thereby averting the possibility of a catastrophic famine. In December the banks were nationalized and the Supreme Council of National Economy formed. Later, foreign trade was nationalized, as were all industrial organizations employing more than five people. Other adopted measures included an eight hour work day, the repudiation of the Tsar's debts, numerous citizen control regulations, and regular confiscations of personal possessions and property. Such were the beginnings of what soon became the greatest slave enterprise in world history. The end result was that a handful of opportunistic, self-appointed leaders subjugated hundreds of millions of people to conditions akin to, if not worse than, slavery. Attempts by the citizens of captive Soviet satellites to rid themselves of Soviet rule were crushed by tanks and troops. Only in Yugoslavia, Rumania and, to a lesser degree Poland, has deviation from the directives of the Supreme Soviet been tolerated, and one can only conjecture why and for how much longer.

In summary, world economic history has witnessed the emergence of five major types of economic systems:

(1) Tribe-Clan;

(2) Master-Slave;

(3) Feudal-Mercantile;

(4) Socialist-Communist;

(5) Capitalist.

Though the first three may be characterized as essentially pre-industrial forms of economic organization, vestiges of their dominant traits remain, affecting us both positively and negatively to this day. But here we are concerned with the last two, capitalism and communism. *Metacapitalism* considers communism, as practiced in the Soviet Union, regressive, a modern reenactment of feudal slavery. *Metacapitalism,* by seeking a maximum personal and financial security for all its citizenry, is thus in opposition to Soviet communism.

The Struggle Between Capitalism and Communism Dominates

It is the struggle between capitalism and communism that will dominate world development and the world economy in both the immediate and the extended future. After more than two million years of human development, we find nothing better than a system characterized by a high degree of relative freedom and little personal or financial security, i.e., capitalism, facing off against a system of Soviet communism that promises vast freedoms for its people but which, in reality, imposes widespread enforced slavery instead. The Soviet Union lowered the Iron Curtain not so much for military security as to contain its vast slave population and keep the horror of this ghastly human spectacle from world view.

It is up to us, if we hope to influence positively the oppressive government of the Soviet Union as it currently exists, to demonstrate by example that freedom is not only highly cherished but also an efficient means for growing an advanced industrial nation and spreading the resulting prosperity to all. In order to comprehend the nature of the threat posed by Soviet communism, it is necessary to get a general sense of the composition of Soviet society and to follow more closely its recent economic development.

OUR KNOWLEDGE OF
THE SOVIET UNION

Before 1950 information about the Soviet Union was as scant as that about Mars, much of the little we had coming from covert activities. Today, although spying continues, we now receive a flood of information through Soviet publications (the accuracy of which is often suspect), the testimony of émigrés, direct contacts, and overhead satellites, which are now so technically sophisticated that they can photograph and transmit the data contained on an automobile's license plate. We know, for instance, that the Soviets are experiencing difficulties holding their farming and peasant populations in check, and that many in their population are educationally overqualified for the positions they hold. We also know that the standard of living for the average Soviet citizen has tripled since 1950, and that Soviet society is a long way from ending up on the "ash heap of history," as was predicted by former President Harry S. Truman. The Soviets are already our military equals. They surpass us in having a thoughtout approach to the future development of their society. If

43

their current economic momentum continues into the intermediate-term future, they will soon achieve economic parity, and then overtake us.

Though we know much about Soviet commodity production, about farm and military production, we know very little about how their leadership makes important decisions or resolves internal conflicts. We know that the Soviet leadership harshly chastises its people for low productivity, for undisciplined and shoddy workmanship, for alcohol abuse, low morality, shady dealing, industrial corruption, pilfering, and cheating. Yet, Soviet leaders will not consider cutting established social programs; neither will they consider introducing even the most rudimentary western freedoms.

The Russian population, excluding satellites, is the most diverse in the world. Its nearly 300 million people speak over one hundred and thirty languages and dialects and occupy 8.6 million square miles, spread over eleven time zones. Yet most of the population, comprising one hundred and four nationalities, is docile, with very low socioeconomic expectations. Years of war and foreign domination, not to mention the cruel tyrannies of the tsars, has left a citizenry numbed and timid. The strategy of the Central Committee of the Communist Party to appease the population with an assortment of social programs like free housing, guaranteed employment, medical care, food and education, a reasonably dignified retirement, seem more than enough.

Employment in the Soviet Union

The Soviet Union is the world's second largest employer after China. About 125 million workers are employed by state owned industries, 20 million by state owned farming and fishing cooperatives, with the remaining 155 million either retired, in school, too young for school or employment, disabled, or imprisoned. Thus, a very high forty seven and one-half percent of the Soviet population is actively, if not voluntarily, engaged in economic production. If students are added to the employment figures, then the figure increases to seventy percent or more of the population.

The Soviet Union as a Classless Society

The Soviet leadership proudly boasts that the U.S.S.R. is a 'classless' society. Yet there are at least seven major classes of citizenship in Russia today. At the very top is the elite leadership, the highest political, military, industrial, and scientific personages, numbering less than 100. The second tier is similarly composed of about 1,000 less important officials. A minor broadening occurs at the third tier, which encompasses top industrial managers, political and professional administrators, senior military and state security officers. These three tiers of Soviet citizenship, numbering in all less than fifteen thousand people, are the upper class, the privileged class, the elite. At the fourth tier the first significant broadening occurs. Here are the several million who compose the upper middle class—college professors, industrial managers, political administrators, Communist Party functionaries, military officers, senior physicians, engineers, and other technologists. In the fifth tier is found the middle class, numbering about 100 million: this is the vast army of industrial workers. At the sixth tier of Soviet society is the lowest class, about 14 million farmers and 'co-opted peasants', a euphemism for slave labor. The seventh tier variously estimated at between 5 and 15 million people, is a grab bag of social and intellectual outcasts, common and political criminals, military prisoners and mental incompetents. This group hangs onto life by the most tenuous of threads and were it not fearful of international recriminations, the Soviet leadership would probably exterminate the entire group.

Communist Party Membership

In the supposedly classless society of the Soviet Union, the Communist Party remains very selective about whom it chooses for membership. Nearly all Soviet elites are members, as are a very small but upwardly mobile percentage of citizens in the fourth and fifth tiers of the society. Fewer than five percent of Soviet citizens are admitted as members of the Communist Party. To refuse the offer is considered highly suspicious and ordinarily leads to an early extinguishment of career prospects. Only members of the Communist Party and their families receive promotions and special privileges, like tickets to the theatre and other cultural events, preferred housing, and special permit shopping.

Personal Possessions in the Soviet Union

Ninety percent of the Soviet population owns no more than a few personal possessions with an aggregate value of no more than a few hundred rubles. (A ruble is roughly equivalent to the American dollar, but as it is not distributed outside of the Soviet Union and its captive satellites, it has no true exchange value). Housing consists of government owned city apartments or rural huts, both cramped and inadequate for the needs of a growing citizenry. Bread and sugar are the food staples. produce availability is steadily improving, and the Soviet consumer has seen the available goods triple since 1950.

Soviet Citizen Control

So fearsome, so intimidating is the policing apparatus of the Soviet State that citizens, from the highest elite to the lowest peasant, cower at the thought of confronting it. Citizens may not speak out against the state or any of its policies; they may not strike or demonstrate in any way. To do so is to court death or an indeterminate

47

sentence in the Gulag. To criticize any aspect of Soviet life in the privacy of one's own dwelling is to risk betrayal by one's closest relatives. The system encourages brother to betray brother, sons and daughters to betray parents. The political indoctrination of Soviet children begins in kindergarten where intra-family suspicion is kindled and valued over family love.

The Struggle For Ideological Supremacy

There is a competition between America and the Soviet Union, a vague struggle for ideological supremacy. The vagueness is not attributable to the motivations or constancy of the battle; the motivations are manifold and the constancy is long standing, changing only from strident to acrimonious in tone. The vagueness is the result of the contradictions that have beset each ideology.

Capitalism is not what it is often accused of being— an unrelenting exploiter of labor and exporter of imperialism. Nor is it particularly characterized by competition and free markets, as economic purists would have you believe. But Soviet communism is not at all what it claims to be; the tyrannical rule of the Soviet leadership is a far cry from the perfect freedom originally prophesied by Marx and Engels.

THE IMMEDIACY OF THE SOVIET ECONOMIC THREAT

The Nature of the Competition Between the US and USSR

The ideological struggle between America and the Soviet Union is evident on many competitive levels. Much attention has been given to the competition for military supremacy, for geopolitical influence, and technological prowess. Until recently the greater threat has remained unseen, namely the growing economic competition between the two countries.

Let no person mislead you. By the end of the twentieth century America's uncertain capitalism is quite likely to be lagging behind Soviet communism in many strategic areas of commodity production. The odds are about fifty-fifty that the Soviets will overtake us, should we manage to sustain our own sluggish long-term rate of economic growth (two to three percent annually), given that no major recessions or depressions occur. Should we experience an economic catastrophe, such as a depression induced by overspeculation or bad investments by our commercial banking industry, the odds shift to become seventy-five to twenty-five in favor of the Soviets, who have all but totally isolated their production system from the risks of the free world economy. At times, it feels as if the Soviets are awaiting just such an ideal opportunity for geopolitical plunder and economic domination.

How the Soviets Have Protected their Economy

The Soviet Union participates in world trade in a highly selective manner, and then only to upset established markets or to gain foreign currency to finance food shortages and their vast overseas intelligence apparatus. Their currency does not trade internationally and is thus free from potentially ruinous international speculation. Soviet imports are limited to items that suit the purposes of the central economic planners, who are careful to avoid any semblance of becoming dependent on foreign production. Unlike our commercial bankers, who have taken it upon themselves to export vast sums of our much-needed working capital in the pursuit of short-term profits, the Soviet central bankers, for the most part, see to it that their capital remains at home. Their shortsightedness has produced not the hoped-for profits but a tense international economic situation in which many developing countries find themselves unable to repay even the interest on their American loans. The list of countries deeply indebted to us and unable to repay grows and grows. Were it not for the intervention of our central bank, several of our largest banks would already have failed, leading to financial chaos and possibly the deep depression for which the Soviets are waiting.

The Competing Economic Systems Described

The world economy of the late twentieth century has many fierce competitors. It is, however, the ideological, economic, and military competition between American capitalism and Soviet communism that is outstanding. Not until recently was the Soviet system of production viewed as a viable competitor to American capitalistic enterprise. Our picture of the Soviets was of an industrially backward country struggling to feed its citizens, while it misspent enormous sums in a meaningless arms race, and advanced a hard line of propaganda about world domination. While our picture of the Soviets has remained fixed, the Soviets, almost imperceptibly over the years, have changed, and their economy has changed along with them.

There has been a significant growth in the Soviet economy. Since 1950 the standard of living for the average Soviet citizen has tripled because Soviet investment in commodity production has shifted conspicuously from industrial production to consumer production. With their material successes in hand, the Soviet threat to rule the world seems to have gained momentum and plausibility. The notion of a unified world communism led by the Soviets has been deflated by the recent actions of the Chinese communists, who have all but removed themselves

51

from the Soviet sphere of authority, and initiated an experiment with rudimentary capitalism. They have now renounced Marxist-Leninist ideology as archaic.

The Soviet Economic Achievement

Much has been said in praise of the West German and Japanese industrial reconstruction and development after World War II. All but forgotten is the massive devastation the Soviets have had to surmount since the end of the war. Considering the economic backwardness of the Soviets at that time, the damage to their people and land, and their mistaken geopolitical wanderlust, the Soviet economic achievement is more remarkable even than that of the Germans or the Japanese. Unfortunately for those who cherish freedom, the economic achievement has provided great impetus to the Soviet military buildup and belligerent Soviet foreign policy. Soviet propaganda, military equipment, and advisors may be found in every corner of the globe. Wherever an internal political crisis appears, it is likely that it has either been instigated by Soviet propagandists, or agitated by Soviet mercenaries. Much of the financing of terrorist organizations may be traced back to the treasury of the Soviet Union and its captive satellites.

The Transformed Nature of the Soviet Threat

Why should Americans care if the Soviet economy overtakes their own? What difference does it make if the

Soviet form of totalitarian communism outproduces American capitalism? On a per capita basis several countries already outproduce us and it has hardly led to dramatic shifts in the world's geopolitical alignments.

Soviet communism represents a highly sophisticated regression in the evolution of political economies. To achieve its current state of economic and military advancement, the elite Soviet leadership has effectively enslaved most of that nation's citizens and the citizenry of its captive satellites as well: hundreds of millions of people in all. By exploiting this vast co-opted pool of labor to the full, and illegally expropriating Western technologies, the Soviets have successfully transformed their economy from being agrarian and backward to being industrialized and advanced in a relatively short period of time. This concerted effort relied much more heavily on totalitarian methods than it did on the ideals of communism. With this authority the Soviet leadership had the obedience of its citizens, whose sense of self had been decimated by the tyranny of the tsars and the devastation and atrocities experienced in the two world wars. Also serving the elite leadership's interests was the richness of Soviet land. Perhaps more important was the still stumbling, bumbling spectacle of America's uncertain capitalism and fatigued democracy.

The Soviet leadership is still smarting over the loss of the People's Republic of China from its sphere of influence and, realistic as it is, knows that our military might and will is more than sufficient to thwart any serious effort of theirs to pursue aggressive military policies. Although an atavistic desire remains in the mentality of the Soviet leadership to export its revolution by military means, the manifestation of that desire has been effectively circumscribed. Americans have served notice upon the Soviets that their sponsorship or active participation in overt or covert military incursions within our sphere of influence will not be tolerated. Added to this has been the Soviet's own experiences in attempting to manage hostile nations. Though the quest for empire still captivates the imperialistic element within their leadership, the Soviets now realize that military dominance over the free world is impossible and they have subtly shifted their attack on the West from the military to the economic arena. So subtle has been this change that Western leaders for the most part have not awakened to it, or, if they have, see it as an idle threat. Even worse, some realize its potential but are incapable of doing anything about it.

The Changing Nature of Commodity Production

Were the world economy still such that the labor component of commodity production was the major component, the Soviet economic threat would be lessened. Both industrial and farm production rely increasingly on advanced technology, such as lasers, fiber optics, robots, machines controlled by computer (CAD—computer aided design, CAM—computer aided manufacturing), microelectronics, microprocessors, biochemistry, and genetic engineering. Just as automated techniques reduced the labor component of manufacturing, heavy equipment, advanced farming techniques, fertilizers, and genetic

engineering are increasing yield per acre and all but rele-
gating the small farmer to technological obsolescence.

Much of human labor in the Soviet Union is forced
and therefore not particularly productive. Forced labor
works only as much as is necessary for subsistence, then
slacks off because incentives and rewards for additional
work are lacking. Soviet agriculture, which until recently
was extremely labor intensive, is a prime example of the
low productivity of forced labor. This is one of the fundamental flaws in the communist conception of society as a
vast co-operative where the principle of egalitarianism
prevails. The Soviets have not learned what the Chinese
communists have, namely that human nature precludes
people from long-term toil solely for the benefit of others
when the benefit to themselves is nil.

Machines Work Without Incentives

Though experience amply demonstrates that people
require incentives to produce beyond mere subsistence,
machines and applied technology do not. If the Soviets
had to rely on labor productivity to achieve their enormous economic growth, they would have failed. Instead,
the Soviets have skillfully reduced the labor component of
their industrial production by importing Western technologies and investing heavily in industrial research. The
combination of a highly automated Soviet Union, rich in
natural resources, skillfully planned and administered by
a motivated technological elite has produced an advanced
industrial society of substance.

THE NEED FOR MACRO-ECONOMIC PLANNING IN AMERICA

Not very long ago, the very idea that the Soviets could overtake the West, particularly America, in the area of commodity production seemed preposterous. Documented accounts of Soviet economic backwardness and production inefficiency were plentiful. There were frequent reports of gigantic production snafus. The efforts of the Soviet central planning apparatus at managerial effectiveness were treated with derision throughout the free world. No one is laughing anymore. The Soviet economic machine is in fine working order. Those who were quick to dismiss central economic planning as an exercise in futility have only demonstrated the depth of their naïveté. Planning has never been an American strength. Our economic enterprise is characterized by crisis management, by reacting to events, rather than by thoughtout approaches to creating the future. We tend to let the future happen and then to work our way out of it or about it. Such an approach is characteristic of chaotic capitalism, of the absence of planning. Effective planning, like almost everything else of consequence, requires a considerable gestation period, a long maturational cycle. Early planning efforts are bound to seem oafish in a short-term contest. Proper planning requires much trial and error, much backing and filling, until an adequate level of planning expertise is reached and sound plans are produced.

In our recent past, when production was dominated by human labor, planning was almost entirely oriented to be short-term. The productive workforce could readily be shifted from one plant to another; it was not the workers' skills so much as their physical presence and labor that was important. But now that our economy has shifted from being labor intensive to being technologically intensive, the need for elaborate planning at the industrial level has become more urgent. The intensity of foreign competition is also accelerating our need for more sophisticated planning at the industrial level. At the national level our economic planning is all but non-existent, possibly a major factor in the stagnation that has afflicted our economy since the decade after World War II. We who had so recently scoffed at the Soviet economy should look at the mess within our own borders.

When on 25 April 1984 the Soviet leader Konstantin U. Chernenko, addressing a commission of the Communist Party's Central Commission in Moscow, claimed that "the reserves of capitalism were far from exhausted" we do not know his motive. Was he attempting to lull Western leaders into a sense of false security? Was this merely another example of Soviet doublespeak? Regarding social, economic, and political progress, America has had a long winter; we have been in near total hibernation since the mid-1960s. Anyone who believes America's uncertain capitalism is still vigorous should look again. Even the economic growth of 1983-5 has been mostly technical, meaning that only a few have benefitted and that no real social progress is at hand. Rather than progress we have regressed under the guise of reducing the federal debt. The conservative government has launched an unprecedented and vitriolic attack upon our people.

What the Soviet Economic Achievement Means To Us

Much as we may choose to ignore it, the vast growth of the Soviet economy has forced the free world, and particularly America, into a long-term competition with extremely high stakes. The outcome will engender significant ideological, economic, and possibly geopolitical ramifications. The Soviet ruling elite has exhibited an appetite for enslavement, for co-opting the labor of its own population, as well as that of conquered territories for its own ends. A Soviet economic victory over the free world could lead to a planet of slaves. America's brand of uncertain capitalism is hardly a viable long-term competitor against the determined onslaught of Soviet communism. Sooner or later capitalism's chaotic, unplanned economic system will give up substantial ground to the Soviet planned system and, at that point, the Soviets will begin to dominate world markets, adding economic might to their ideological arsenal.

US/USSR . . . Comparative Economic Statistics;
Strengths and Weaknesses

With uncharacteristic candor, the Soviet leadership admits periodically to an intense and critical economic competition with the West and particularly with the United States. They view the competition as a decisive crusade, a victory being final proof that Soviet communism is superior to American capitalism.

Given the gravity of the situation our leadership is uncharacteristically quiet, even hushed. We hope they are neither dumbstruck nor dumbfounded, but their feeble responses to the Soviet economic challenge leave us distressed by our seeming inability to acknowledge and either formally respond to or dismiss the Soviet economic threat.

Following is a comparison of American and Soviet commodity production for the twenty-four years from 1960 to 1983, as assembled by the Directorate of Intelligence of our Central Intelligence Agency (CIA). These figures present a picture, not of a bumbling and bungling Soviet economy, but rather of a dynamic economic machine that has produced an extensive economic miracle in a barren, war-torn land. Far from being exhausted, this country has launched a steady and so far successful mis-

COMMODITY PRODUCTION: US VS. USSR*

Commodity	1960	1983	Commodity	1960	1983
Primary energy (million b/d of oil equivalent)			Trucks and buses (millions)		
US	21.1	30.8	US	1.2	3.7
USSR	9.2	29.2	USSR	0.4	0.9
Crude oil (thousand b/d)			Cement (million metric tons)		
US	7,055	8,680	US	56.1	63.9
USSR	2,943	11,864	USSR	45.5	128.0
Natural gas (trillion cubic feet)			Grain (million metric tons)		
US	12.8	16.6	US	181.3	208.5
USSR	1.6	18.9	USSR	125.6	195.0
Hard coal (million metric tons)			Wheat (million metric tons)		
US	391.5	658.9	US	36.9	66.0
USSR	355.9	486.0	USSR	64.3	78.0
Brown coal and lignite (million metric tons)			Coarse grain (million metric tons)		
US	2.5	53.1	US	141.9	138.0
USSR	134.2	159.0	USSR	61.1	105.0
Electricity (billion kilowatt-hours)			Potatoes (million metric tons)		
US	893.7	2,459.2	US	11.7	14.8
USSR	292.3	1,416.4	USSR	84.4	83.0
Iron ore (million metric tons)			Sugar (million metric tons)		
US	90.2	38.6	US	3.6	5.2
USSR	105.9	245.0	USSR	6.9	13.6
Bauxite (thousand metric tons)			Meat (million metric tons)		
US	2,030	662	US	12.8	25.0
USSR	3,100	8,900	USSR	8.7	16.0

(continued)

Commodity	1960	1983	Commodity	1960	1983
Pig iron (million metric tons)			Milk (million metric tons)		
US	62.2	44.2	US	53.7	63.5
USSR	46.8	110.0	USSR	61.7	96.4
Crude steel (million metric tons)			Ginned cotton (thousand metric tons)		
US	90.1	75.6	US	3,107	1,682
USSR	65.3	153.0	USSR	1,458	2,700
Refined copper (thousand metric tons)			Mineral fertilizer (million metric tons, nutrient content)		
US	1,650	1,613	US[b]	7.4	18.0
USSR	475	1,540	USSR	3.3	29.7
Primary aluminum (thousand metric tons)			Nitrogen fertilizer (million metric tons of N)		
US	1,827	3,353	US[b]	2.5	8.7
USSR	565	2,795	USSR	1.0	13.0
Lead (thousand metric tons)			Plastics (million metric tons)		
US	347	515	US	2.8	14.0
USSR	300	565	USSR	0.3	4.4
Refined zinc (thousand metric tons)			Synthetic rubber (million metric tons)		
US	788	302	US	1.5	2.0
USSR	360	825	USSR	0.3	1.8
Gold (million troy ounces)			Tractors (thousands)		
US	1.7	1.6	US	178.5	91.6
USSR	3.6	10.7	USSR	238.5	564.0
Synthetic ammonia (million metric tons of N)			Automobiles (millions)		
US	3.6	10.0	US	6.7	6.7
USSR	1.1	16.8	USSR	0.1	1.3

*Figures above extracted from the Central Intelligence Agency's "Handbook of Economic Statistics, 1984."

61

sion to overtake the United States as the world's chief producer of goods and services.

For Karl Marx, writing over a century ago, the central distinction between capitalism and communism was property. Marx attached much evil to the private ownership of property and particularly to the private ownership of the means of production. The fledgling capitalism he so loathed was every bit as onerous as he depicted it. Since then capitalism has evolved for the better. The harshly exploitative practices of America's frontier capitalists were fortunately tempered by the growth in the power of worker's unions and the ubiquitous influence of the Industrial Revolution, which all but displaced human labor as an important component of industrial production. Today, Soviet communists, the possessors of all of Russia's public property, the owners of all of the means of production, even small tools, are far more cruel, far more loathsome exploiters of human labor than the worst of the American frontier capitalists.

Whether property be private or public, however, is not the central issue at the beginning of the twenty-first century. The Soviets have proved beyond the shadow of a doubt that it is not property, but rather the nature of the principles that guide government that determines the fate of a nation's citizenry. In America, the overdeveloped concern for property rights has served to retard our social, economic, and political progress. In the Soviet Union, the lack of regard for human rights has served to retard economic development. Both nations are growing and will continue to grow, but both nations are suffering from confusions that retard the pace of their respective advances.

By far the greatest economic distinction between the United States and the Soviet Union is the relative freedoms accorded individuals and businesses to pursue economic activities. The differences between America's current uncertain capitalism and the Soviet's phantom communism are as extreme as night and day.

Ours is a market society, often mislabeled a "free market society." Much of economic activity—what we build, what we purchase, interest rates, wages and salaries, commodity prices— is purportedly determined by the market and the interaction of forces that economists have labeled supply and demand. Our citizens are, for the most part, free to pursue any business or occupation that pleases them. Their success or failure in their chosen pursuit will usually be determined by their ability to compete effectively with others. For instance, should a person or group decide to manufacture white athletic socks, they will find that a variety of market prices, for capital, for labor, for raw materials, and the like. If they wish to sell their socks they will have to do so at the market price or convince potential buyers that their socks are worth a higher price. American business people who are unable to compete at the market price or attract a higher price are soon forced to pursue other interests, usually suffering a modest to extensive loss of personal capital. Those Americans with extraordinary abilities, initiative, talents, skills, inventive and innovative genius, organizational, entrepreneurial or artistic capacities, may earn princely sums in the market. Though the average American earns $15,000-$30,00 per annum, many others earn $50,000-$250,000. At the very top of the income pyramid are the few who command more than $100,000,000 each year. The American market economy suffers from a variety of ills: unequal opportunity, monopoly, corruption, government interference, managerial incompetence, and industrial inefficiency. On the whole, however, it provides an environment flush with incentives for individual endeavor.

The Soviet economic system is not driven by free market forces. All but the least significant Soviet economic activity is rigidly controlled by the state, which owns all of the means of production. Soviet state economic control ensues from the totalitarian powers vested in the Soviet leadership, the Supreme Soviet. Industrial investment, industrial output, the prices of all goods and services, wage and salary levels, production quantities, specific units of production—all are established by a variety of state planning authorities that together comprise the Gosplan, which itself derives its authority from the Supreme Soviet Economic Council. There is substantial interaction between Soviet industries and the various levels of the state planning organizations, but in the end what is produced as well as its price and quantity and the level of wages and salaries are not set by competitive market forces, but by the authority of the Supreme Soviet, as delegated to the Supreme Economic Council, the regional and local planning committees and, finally to the industries, and workers themselves.

As with most planned systems, Soviet economic control was at first rudimentary, awkward and fraught with inefficiencies. Practice has produced many refinements and Soviet central planning activities, once seemingly inefficient are not institutionally entrenched, and continuing to grow in effectiveness and sophistication. Working together, the appropriate sections of the Gosplan and the Gosbank (the single Soviet banking authority) administer the money supply and approve or disapprove specific plans for creating new or expanding old Soviet industries. Soviet citizens may submit plans for new business enterprises (called projects) to the Gosbank for financing, but the Soviet 'entrepreneur' may participate in the growth and profits of the enterprise only to the degree permitted by the State.

The strict authoritarianism of the Soviet State over economic affairs has enabled the leadership to divert an extraordinary percentage of economic activity away from consumer-oriented production and into industrial and military production. This emphasis on industrial production, fueled by the sacrifices forced on the Soviet citizenry, has paid off handsomely for those who stand in opposition to capitalism, freedom, and democracy.

Soviet ideologies claim that substituting state ownership, domination, and control for private property, ownership, and control of the means of production, will produce a classless society. A society that is classless is, according to these ideologies, a better society. In such a society class struggles vanish and farmers, bureaucrats, skilled and unskilled workers, managers, teachers, artists, and even intellectuals live and work side by side in a state of perpetual bliss. But are we permitted to examine, close up and, without interference, the remote cities and the countryside, and the people who constitute this vast classless society? Clearly, we are denied such access. Why? Contrary to the pronouncements of the Soviet propagandists we find a class structure replete with fine gradations of rank and privilege. We find several hundred million impoverished peasants at forced labor, held in check not by ideology but by a powerful domestic police force that is armed to the teeth. The purported blissful state is, in fact, a brutal, totalitarian, police state which uses every known form of coercion, intimidation, and consciousness control (propaganda and misinformation) to terrorize the peasantry into submission.

In the Soviet Union freedom has been reduced to a useless axiom: the Soviet state is free to impose its will on its citizenry and the citizenry is free to obey the dictates of the state. All human activity emanates from the authority of the Supreme Soviet, and citizens who clash with or attempt to reshape or reform state policy or practice, or who express their dissent in any way are quickly dealt with, labeled as socially flawed, criticized, ostracized, imprisoned, or murdered.

The Soviet leadership has pushed its people hard. The result has been an enormous development of physical infrastructure, industrial production, and military acceleration. Their authoritarian system substitutes fear for monetary incentive and, though fear is a not inconsiderable motivating force, it tends to produce plodders rather than innovators. Without monetary incentive for economic achievement, Soviet managers are more persevering than entrepreneurial, more apt to push the increase of an existing enterprise than to suggest new enterprises—sluggish drudges rather than spirited transmogrifiers.

Were it not for free world technological innovation and our willingness to export our machinery to them, the swagger and bluster that marks the Soviet leadership would dissolve into agrarian backwardness.

If the spirit of entrepreneurship in the Soviet Union is thwarted by the lack of financial inducements, in America we are afflicted by an agglutination of entrepreneurial disincentives, running the gamut from the purposeful sabotage by the entrenched wealthy to the miserable bumbling of a well-intentioned leadership. All told, the continuing successes of American uncertain capitalism ought to rank as one of the seven wonders of the world. We overspeculate, we underplan, we overregulate, we monopolize and oligopolize, we bureaucratize and we imperialize, we export needed working capital and import defaulted loans, we pump billions into failed companies and industries and neglect to fund emerging entrepreneurs. America's uncertain capitalism is a once vibrant person whose will remains intact but whose already deteriorating bodily functions are made all the worse by a multitude of economists and politicians who display the characteristics of hobbits rather than master physicians. If we are to win the

economic competition with the Soviets, our leadership
must shun our archaic, economic legerdemain and confront our deep-rooted structural problems, rather than
continuously applying cosmetic lotions to the surface.

We are a free market economy competing with an
increasingly well-managed state economy. In a free market economy, a well-managed firm will usually outcom-
pete a poorly managed firm. Thus, if we are to win our
economic competition with the Soviets, we must somehow transform our undermanaged free market economy
into a well managed free market economy. We must find
an industrial policy that is consistent with freedom and
the best ingredients of capitalism; we must remove all
unnecessary impediments to the market's various mechanisms; we must ensure that the market's physical and
institutional infrastructure is well maintained and modernized and we must rid it of the instruments of monopolism and corruption.

The Soviets' greatest strength is not their authoritarian economic system but rather their sense of national
purpose, their dogged commitment to the achievement of
national economic objectives. Whether convinced or
forced, the Soviet people have long sacrificed personal
comfort for national economic progress. The Soviets manufacture tractors, not automobiles, machinery to build
more machinery, not trinkets and cosmetics. Theirs is a
professional government, ours a government populated
predominantly by self-interested amateurs. The Soviets
have effectively isolated their economy from the vicissi-

tudes of international, business cycles. We have become immersed in self-defeating exploitative foreign lending practices.

Someone in our State Department wasn't on duty when the commercial bankers usurped their functions and powers.

US/USSR Positive and Negative Economic Conditions In Common

The United States and the Soviet Union share important economic conditions. Each is rich with a wide variety of natural resources, including ore, farmland, ports, oil, and timber. It is highly unlikely that America would have developed as rapidly as it did during the Industrial Revolution had it not been for the expeditious discovery (financed by Andrew Carnegie, but led by an Indian guide named Majigijig) of vast deposits of high grade iron ore in northern Minnesota, later named the Mesabi Range. Nor is it likely that Soviet industrial development could progress without the rich diversity of their mineral resources, particularly iron ore and oil. Each contains an enormous and culturally diverse population, a vast industrial and educational network and each is now relatively secure from external invasion or destabilizing internal rebellion.

On the negative side, each is afflicted by the remnants of archaic ideologies, bloated bureaucracies, and intransigent institutional infrastructures. Neither capitalism nor communism as practiced in America or the Soviet Union is what it ought to be and, as matters are developing, the ambiguities that afflict each system detract from its future development, threatening the safety of the world's citizenry.

Part III

THE NATURE OF AMERICAN CAPITALISM: WHY IT IS UNCERTAIN

CAPITALISM FROM *METACAPITALISM'S* PERSPECTIVE

Modern democracy originated in America, capitalism did not. Capitalism sprang up in so many places, in so many guises and at so many different times that at least a few priggish historians refuse to recognize it as a significant historical event. Perhaps they are correct. Capitalism was not a revolutionary replacement for some other form of economic system, nor was it legitimized by government constitution or decree. Capitalism has never been formalized into a consistent economic doctrine for commercial and industrial development.

The term capitalism was probably coined by Karl Marx, of all people, who understood its historical development and ultimate consequence better than anyone before him and most after him. All we can state definitively is that capitalism first emerged in Europe during the thirteenth century, if not earlier. The study of capitalism is disquietingly like studies of early man—despite prodigious amounts of conjecture, the precise origins of man and capitalism are perhaps forever shrouded in darkness.

However, there is a matter on which the majority of historians agree: Capitalism is the economic system which superceded feudalism. Sociologists perceive capitalism as an ongoing, complex, historical process with various social, religious, political and ideological roots. Economists seem uncertain about how they ultimately wish to define capitalism. Those few who do address capitalism's history usually do so by dredging up the work of classical economics' early giants, namely Adam Smith (1723-1790), Thomas Robert Malthus (1766-1834), David Ricardo (1772-1823), and John Stuart Mill (1806-1873). In view of the common nationality of all of these men, the heavily British orientation of modern economists vis-à-vis the origins of capitalism is hardly surprising. Even Karl Marx did most of his writing in exile, in England. Politicians, who express an interest in the theory and origins of capitalism, but who are too busy or too confused by its convolutedness, hire economists to sort it out for them, the majority of whom are just as confused and perplexed.

For the purposes of this revolutionary primer it is sufficient to define capitalism as an economic system that evolved in Europe alongside feudalism, ultimately replacing it, because of its superior productive potential.

New economic systems can evolve in the wake of increasing productivity or, alternatively, as the result of social, economic, and political experimentation. Regardless of the nature of their origins, history amply demonstrates that economic systems must compete among themselves. No free citizenry will tolerate a stagnant or deteriorating economic environment, particularly when other options are available. In the long-run the efficient system is bound to replace the inefficient one.

Today feudalism appears to have been an oppressive and coercive economic system. It was however, a definite step forward from the slave economy which preceded it. The slave masters of the early Middle Ages were markedly more tyrannical than their feudal successors. Slaves had no rights; they could not possess property or establish households, and could be legitimately tortured, starved, or murdered. At least serfs gained limited legal protection. They were encouraged to establish households by their overlords. However, both serfs and slaves could be bought and sold by their masters, and neither was free to move about the countryside, change occupation or master. Thus, although serfdom was an advance over slavery, it was certainly no quantum leap. Serfs were, on the whole, offered more incentives to be productive, but, their standard of living and productivity, compared to modern times, were dismal.

It is important here to emphasize that one economic system may be said to have replaced another economic system only when the new system has become the dominant force in the organization, production, and distribution of a nation's resources. During the period of transition from one system to another, most important economic transactions will move from the old system to the new with increasing speed. It is not until the new system has all but totally replaced the old that the new economic era should be announced.

THE NATURE AND GROWTH OF AMERICAN CAPITALISM

Although capitalism took root in Europe long before America was settled, it seems perfectly appropriate today to think of capitalism, the Industrial Revolution, and American democracy as inseparable. Capitalism began to establish itself in America with the onset of the Industrial Revolution, which had spread with the immigrants from Europe, towards the end of the eighteenth century. This *revolution*, (ongoing even today), transformed America with a ferocity never before encountered in history from an agrarian society into an advanced industrial nation. Breaking from a static worldview, the Industrial Revolution created dynamism. People whose position in life was relatively fixed could now look forward to vast improvements. Social mobility became a reality as an enormous middle class emerged in America. As more and more people left rural communities, seeking opportunity in the burgeoning cities, the nation's population soared from 40 million in 1870 to 205 million in 1970, an increase of over four hundred percent in only a century. Even more extraordinary was the per capita growth in production and income. During the same century the gross national product grew a startling 13,860 percent from $7 billion to $977 billion, the gross national product per capita rose 2,600 percent from $175 to $4,766 in 1970 constant dollars.

Yet, America's first settlers were not capitalists, but rather a mixed array of British aristocracy who were bequeathed land, a large contingent of families seeking release from religious persecution, and an assortment of adventurers, explorers, criminals, and slaves. The America of the sixteenth, seventeenth, and eighteenth centuries was a highly mixed feudal/agrarian/mercantile society. It was not until the inventions of the eighteenth century took hold in the nineteenth century that America was wholly converted to capitalism. Before that, ours was an eclectic economy, an exotic mixture of enterprising farmers, frontiersmen, small proprietors, hucksters, and traders.

The inventive process long preceded the industrial application of new machines and the final evolution of capitalism as America's dominant economic system. The dreams and drawings of Leonardo da Vinci (1452-1519), painter, sculptor, architect, engineer, and scientist, began emerging into reality in the late sixteenth century. There was William Lee's stocking-frame in 1598, Dudley's patent for making iron with pit coal, Cort's iron oxidizing process and rolling mill in 1784, the predecessors of James Watt's steam engine of 1769, Savery's steam condensing engine of 1698, Newcomen's atmospheric engine of 1712, Kay's flying shuttle of 1733. A series of inventions transformed the cotton industry; the spinning-jenny by Hargreaves in 1770, the water-frame by Arkwright in 1769, Kelly's self-acting mule in 1792, Crompton's mule in 1779, and Cartwright's power-loom in 1785, coal smelting, and the application of the steam engine to blast furnaces.

The capitalism of today, however, is very different from that of the nineteenth century. The very machines that were so instrumental in luring America's population away from farms and into cities, offering urban employment opportunities to the young and freeing them from the rigors and uncertainty of farm life, now hold our nation's citizenry in an economic stranglehold of dependency. Americans have grown accustomed to the various employments offered by our current economic system—so accustomed that many American workers can no longer fend for themselves when unemployment strikes, as it has in many of our primary industries, such as automobiles, steel, aluminum, farm equipment, and textiles.

Long ago large segments of our citizenry gave up their individual trades and tools in favor of industrial employment. Considering the times and the inducements, theirs was an appropriate decision. Increases in the production of goods created a major rise in the production of educational, medical, and union services, which led to the significant increases in the standard of living that the majority of Americans have experienced since the late eighteenth century. This historical economic achievement is perhaps best personified in the rise of the middle class. However, the very machinery that uplifted vast numbers of our people, that helped free them from their parochial existences, now threatens each and every one of us.

Questioning Capitalism Today

How are we to understand America's miraculous economic transformation in light of today's problems? Why is it imperative for us to root out the factors responsible for America's early economic success? The closest our technical economists can come to explaining what happened in America is to praise our free market system, laud the accomplishments of our early entrepreneurs and pioneers, honor our predominantly laissez-faire, profit-driven corporate system, commend the work ethic, praise our inventiveness and managerial expertise, eulogize Keynes and Franklin D. Roosevelt for rescuing us from the Great Depression, and, on occasion, to credit American machines and natural resources. While such nostalgic sentimentalism is flattering, it fails as an analytical framework from which a future course, with appropriate correctives, for the American economy may be drawn.

Two prodigious essences form the bedrock of our societal success. These are machinery and freedom. Machines, a co-opted peasantry, and an authoritarian government fuel the advance of the Soviet economic system, while machines and a relatively free citizenry fuel capitalism. What distinguishes capitalism from communism is its free citizenry. In America, our national anthem defines America as "the land of the free and the home of the brave." A free people, free markets, a freely elected government, these are the forces that have energized American capitalism.

Pure capitalism, divorced from the influence of politics and government, exists only in the minds and texts of students of economics. Pure capitalism, according to how most economists would define it today, would manifest competition, markets free from government tariffs and regulations, and nearly universal private ownership of the means of production and distribution. Such staunch supporters of pure capitalism are an interesting but grossly inconsistent and ignorant lot. Among them may be found those who would readily take upon themselves the dubious appellation of social Darwinists. They are our rugged individualists who preach the survival of the fittest, decrying the poor and the handicapped as impediments to the progress of capitalistic society. They are the harshest critics of governmental assistance to the needy, of social reform, and the advance of a just society. They bemoan governmental assistance, even as they spend their unearned inheritances; they bemoan the so-called slippage in the American work ethic, but do not fear the influence of the bequests to their heirs. The social Darwinist is anathema to humanism and a dinosaur in **Metacapitalism's** world. Their thoughts are transplants from another age, when Americans were struggling to achieve a national identity, to free themselves from the inglorious fate of being a British colony, to form a new government, and to settle a new land.

The historic freedoms that we so cherish today are threatened by our failure to update our thinking, in order to respond to contemporary social problems. We are presently living in a post-industrial age, with an increasingly alienated and disenfranchised service class, to whom the fundamental freedoms are increasingly denied. We must move beyond the articulation of verbal truisms to effective action. Freedom of speech and press, for instance, are glorious freedoms we should protect. Yet, they have little more than indirect value today for the many without the skills or platform to use them. Our right to life, liberty, and the pursuit of happiness will soon be no more than empty words. Only through examining, developing, and then deploying programs that will produce in America as just a society as possible, given the constraints of limited resources, our propensity for self-interest, and the triple-edged Soviet threat, will we rise above the stagnation and mediocrity besetting us. Then we will serve again as a positive model for all the world.

America emerged from World War II as an attractive world center. After unqualified military victories in the Atlantic and the Pacific, American capitalism was in high gear, with per capita income rising from $758 in 1940, $1525 in 1945, to $1887 in 1950. Headed by President Harry S. Truman, a confident post-war government passed the Full Employment Act of 1946, assuring our citizenry that no more than a small percentage of our population would ever become unemployed without the federal government deploying its economic might to rectify the situation.

We were fat and happy. Our soldiers, sailors, and aviators returned to the home workforce to vastly improved wages. Many profited greatly from the war, especially heavy industry and growing technological fields. The unions swelled with members and gained national recognition. America was the envy of all the world. It was for many a Golden Age. The rich continued to grow richer, while the middle class continued to believe in the American Dream, and their income steadily rose. To most of the world, the American lifestyle seemed unbelievably blessed with material wealth. Americans could own a suburban house, furnish it well with mass produced furniture, place a car or two in the garage, and send some, if not all, of their children to college.

Today many Americans are still driven by these modest goals. Compared with the poverty afflicting most of the world, a house, furniture, appliances, a job, and an education represent an elevation of the human condition. And yet, today we realize that many nations have greatly surpassed our material standards. The Scandinavian societies, Canada, New Zealand, many European countries, and Australia have already surpassed them, with the Japanese and the Soviets not far behind. In fact, the case could be made that the Soviets have already passed us.

What has gone wrong? Why is America stagnating? What is the nature of our malaise? Analysis and theories abound. There are shock theorists who attribute our economic and social ills to Watergate, Vietnam, the OPEC price war, or the Iranian hostage crisis. These events, though sensational and disruptive, potentially debilitating in the short run, have very little to do with the overall success and productivity of our nation. That we time and again persevere through such storms only serves to strengthen us. Even our worst crises, such as the massive deprivation and social dislocation suffered during the Great Depression, or the heavy casualties of World War II, Korea and Vietnam, served only to unify and make the American people more resilient. Shock theory, therefore, is not a convincing explanation of the growing American economic and social malaise.

UNCERTAIN CAPITALISM: A SWAMP OF MEDIOCRITY

Alongside the shock theorists stand numerous others, each armed with an arsenal of reasons for our stagnation. Without affixing labels, we shall attempt to list those which seem to carry the greatest weight, and whose supporters are most vocal. Lately, it is the federal deficit, heavy defense spending, lagging productivity, aggressive competition from abroad, high interest rates, nagging unemployment, an incompetent banking system, our negative balance of payments, and a diminished work ethic that have taken the brunt of the blame. Not long ago, analysts of our malaise pinpointed inflation, stagflation, our stop-and-go economy, an excess of social spending, underinvestment in our basic industries, excessive consumer debt, conspicuous consumption, the size of government, the unchecked dominance of the unions, and a general feeling of uncertainty as the true factors underlying our malaise. Supply-side economists blame the demand-oriented Keynesians; the poor and the middle classes blame the wealthy; domestic chauvinists blame the internationalists; Democrats blame Republicans; farmers blame city slickers; blacks blame whites; women blame men; unions blame management. By continuously bickering among ourselves, by tossing the ball from one court to another, we deflect our vision from the true nature of our social and economic malaise.

It is a fundamental belief of **Metacapitalism** that America's economic and social malaise is attributable to our uncertain capitalism, or in other words, to our economic system that was never truly thoughtout. What went wrong in America? Nothing. Things were never really right. Beginning as a poor relative in a colonial empire, as foreign invaders, as monstrous abusers of slaves and Indians, as a misbegotten lot of adventurers, religious reactionaries, lost souls, and assorted fools, we barely managed to piece together a revolution freeing us from British domination, to write a Constitution and to form a government. Though the new government was barely able to hold its head above water, considering the times, the Constitution and the later Bill of Rights were marvels. True, they left much unsaid and much open to interpretation. The rights of slaves, of women, and of Indians were ignored. Broad freedoms were defined, which are now so familiar that we have come to take them for granted. Freedom of religion, of speech and of publication were, at the time, remarkable.

Yet, along with these much heralded rights, there were freedoms that weren't highly proclaimed. There was the freedom of the sick to die unattended for want of funds for medical attention; there was the freedom to live in the streets, or under bridges for lack of money; there was the freedom to scrounge in the streets for food; to be sentenced for uncommitted crimes; to be fired from your job without any compensation; to be grossly exploited by employers; to earn a wage barely sufficient to keep you alive; to work in unsafe conditions, unsuitable even for animals; to be excluded from opportunity because you were a member of a minority, or a woman, disfigured, disabled, or elderly. Veterans who fought to protect our freedoms, and who lost limbs in the process, were free to beg in the streets. There was the freedom of those born mentally or physically handicapped to lead lives of utter and desperate frustration. These and a host of other freedoms are not much trumpeted, as are those portrayed so wonderfully in our founding documents. Yet, different as these two sets of freedoms are, they share a common feature. They were born together, fraternal twins; they were raised together and they co-exist today. There have been some changes, but nothing very significant. There are those who wish to abridge even our much heralded freedoms. They are an unimportant minority; their fire will soon die. There are many more who choose to ignore our other freedoms; not held so dearly—despair, poverty, hunger, prejudice, exploitation, corruption, powerlessness, disease, incapacity, injustice. Who are the many who ignore these freedoms? None but you and me, the American majority. With a brilliance that defies description, we have been shaped into an uncaring, undoing, unfeeling, unseeing, docile mass. It was said that "the American majority has been an amiable shepherd dog kept forever on a lion's leash." The confusions and contradictions that together fashion our current uncertain capitalism are our lion's leash. The bloated bureaucracy that is our federal government is our lion's leash. Our archaic system of representative government is our lion's leash. Our rotting physical infrastructure is our lion's leash. Our distorted institutional infrastructure is our lion's leash. Our helter-skelter capitalism is our lion's leash. Our corrupt government is our lion's leash. Our unbelievably timid economic programs and policies are our lion's leash. The fact that our citizenry has somehow settled for the role of gentle shepherd dog . . . this is our lion's leash.

Metacapitalism seeks to awaken the American people from its long slumber. Uncertainty arises from inaction or wrong actions. Only action vanquishes uncertainty. *Metacapitalism* seeks to increase the tempo of social, economic, and political innovation in America. *Metacapitalism* seeks to remove the lion's leash from the amiable shepherd dog. *Metacapitalism* seeks to expose the economic myths that underlie our uncertain capitalism. *Metacapitalism* will propose new and sweeping programs for transforming America. Were *Metacapitalism* now in place the difference in America would be as startling as the difference between America today and feudal Europe in the Middle Ages. Verbal eugenics will not get the job done. Excessive speechmaking is misconstrued as justice and thus threatens and impedes it. The 435 speechmakers in the House of Representatives are prime examples of how government grows too large and cumbersome to serve the general interest and thus thwarts it by stifling the tempo of economic, social, and political experimentation.

THE UNCERTAINTY IN UNCERTAIN CAPITALISM

It is unfair, perhaps unjust, to label American capitalism as uncertain without clearly setting forth a bill of particulars, an impartial indictment, a list of its fundamental problems. The preparation of such a list must, of course, be tempered by the philosophical perspective of the *preparer*. That perspective is an excited, impatient, and expectant humanitarianism.

What makes uncertain capitalism unstable? There are ten major problem areas, flaws, faults. They are:

1. Uncertain capitalism has evinced a contemptuous, disdainful and even arrogant disregard for those Americans who do not fit the image of the rugged individualist, or who were not born to or have somehow accumulated wealth. Given the great wealth, resources, and inventiveness of our society, uncertain capitalism has been wantonly negligent in its avoidance of the articulation and implementation of a modern Bill of Rights for the American people. From **Metacapitalism's** per-

spective such rights or entitlements would necessarily include income security, retirement security, medical security, legal security, and educational security. In subsequent chapters these various securities which must be posited as elementary in an advanced industrial society are delineated in greater detail.

2. Uncertain capitalism is capitalism that has resisted modernization. It has refused to update its version of our historical and cherished freedoms. In just the same way, it has avoided confronting the fundamental issue of employment in a changing economy. *Metacapitalism* will argue that it is necessary to restructure our traditional ideals to cope with a changing world.

3. Uncertain capitalism almost ignores the importance of American communities. Community service, which is close to the hearts of many of our citizens, both young and old, active and sedentary, is not given sufficient priority, and thus, is stymied for lack of an appropriate infrastructure. *Metacapitalism* proposes a partly compulsory community service program for those who are about to enter a university, and a part voluntary program for those who wish to donate a portion of their time towards the betterment of their communities.

4. Uncertain capitalism seems altogether unprepared to deal fairly with the concept of justice.

Our archaic set of laws, which overwhelmingly favors the rich and disdains the poor and the middle classes is a disgraceful, ignominious mockery. *Metacapitalism* proposes a preliminary set of judicial principles to guide future thinking about restoring a sense of justice and reality to our anachronistic legal procedures.

5. Uncertain capitalism and unequal opportunity are nearly synonymous. Even a partial list of the inequalities that persist and are enhanced by uncertain capitalism soon begins to become lengthy. A fundamental tenet of *Metacapitalism* is the recognition that inequalities resulting from family inheritance should not be further exacerbated by inappropriate economic policy, an elitist body of law, or inadequate social financing. Each program or policy conceived and advanced under *Metacapitalism* promotes the general interest and helps tear down the barriers to equal opportunity for our entire citizenry.

6. Uncertain capitalism is riddled with dubious economic policies and seriously flawed by its dependence on classical and neo-classical economic theory. Among the economic items *Metacapitalism* will propose are a national industrial strategy and economic plan, a linking of the money supply to an extrapolated projection of economic growth, a permanently lowered maximum rate of interest, the notion of a consumer class, a reitera-

tion of capitalism's need for mass markets—a domestic citizenry with an expanding purchasing power.

7. Uncertain capitalism is also riddled with an increasingly rabid speculative fever. Overspeculation has taken us to the brink of what could prove to be a catastrophic world depression, an event with such ghastly prospects that only the outbreak of a nuclear war seems more grim. *Metacapitalism*, under the aegis of corporate and financial reform, will propose a reorganization of our banking system and financial markets to reduce the risks of a speculation induced depression.

8. Uncertain capitalism is aided and abetted by our bloated government bureaucracy. Genuine efforts to reduce uncertainty, to broaden entitlements, to reduce complexity, to introduce efficiency, to respond to the needs of the poor and middle classes are thwarted by the well financed reactionary interests that dominate our political processes. Government for the few instead of for the many need not be tolerated. Ways and means exist within our current laws to remedy these distortions. They should be used, and if these are not enough, new laws should be proposed and enacted. *Metacapitalism* will exhume and illuminate the existing process for massive political change, for moving from our archaic system

of representative government to a system directed by the votes of the citizenry instead of the self-interest of politicians. Only when our citizens have a direct interest in issues and an ability to translate that interest into political action via their votes will capitalism receive the full strength and support of the American people.

9. Uncertain capitalism is a confused mixture of ideas, beliefs, customs, traditions, mores, superstitions, conformities, orthodoxies, decorums, etiquettes, contrivances, myths, legends, folklore, observances, compliances, adaptations, habits, and bureaucracies that have collected over the years to give us our thoroughly clogged institutional infrastructure. It is this multifaceted institutional infrastructure that inhibits the poor and middle classes from active participation in our economic, social, and political processes. *Metacapitalism* will propose a variety of programs and policies for unblocking our vital resources.

10. Uncertain capitalism is extraordinarily timorous in its approach to economic, social, and political experimentation. Its restraint in these areas is more than matched by its resolve to protect private property. It does not require an overly keen eye to note the stamp of the idle rich on much of the legislation and business passed by Congress. Above all else, the wealthy suffer from a fanatical

fear of confiscation of their property, attacks from violent insurrectionists or rebellious malcontents, the development of a society where servants and workers are scarce, and physical proximity with anyone not of their class. **Metacapitalism** shares with capitalism an affinity for the virtues of private property, but these must be balanced by the general needs of our society.

In just one small section of his brilliant and beautiful poem, *The People, Yes,* Carl Sandburg captures the essence of the frustrations suffered by those confronted by the inequities of inherited property.

"Get off this estate."
"What for?"
"Because it's mine."
"Where did you get it?"
"From my father."
"Where did he get it?"
"From his father."
"And where did he get it?"
"He fought for it."
"Well I'll fight you for it."

In Andrew Carnegie's memoirs there is an illuminating section on the true qualities of vibrant capitalism. One such quality is that under capitalism an exaggerated quantity of wealth adheres to the successful capitalist. Carnegie considered the capitalist who amassed great wealth a temporary custodian of that money. On his death the wealth would naturally be transferred back to society. *Metacapitalism* shares Carnegie's view of inheritance and proposes laws to foreclose the possibility of America's further development into a country ruled by and for a constitutional aristocracy.

For too long we have stagnated, resting on our laurels, victims of complacency, as the Soviet economy has overtaken our own. Are we willing to be vanquished by an enslaved citizenry, tyrannically directed by a central committee? Has something terrible destroyed the competitive and idealistic spirit of Americans?

On the other hand, perhaps we will find that the much discussed complacency of our citizenry will vanish once *Metacapitalism's* menu, filled with appetizing choices, is before them.

Almost all Americans, the very wealthy excepted, live their entire lives in a completely vulnerable position. The already great gulf between rich and poor is wider with each passing day. Must it be that the vast majority of Americans live in fear of unemployment, of financial ruin should they fall seriously ill, or of not having sufficient funds to finance their children's education? We no longer live a frontier existence. We must not succumb to the monolithic moralizing of the entrenched status quo which seeks to return to the dark ages of our economic past with their pockets filled, of course, with modern-day plunder. Not individualism but individual initiative mixed with mutual dependency is the reality of the human condition within advanced industrial societies.

WHY WE SHOULD CONCERN
OURSELVES WITH OUR ECONOMY

For a full quarter of a century, the American citizenry has heard much of our problems without hearing concrete proposals for resolving them. While those erstwhile guardians of the American status quo have governed us into an unconscious complacency, we have witnessed the rise of an aggressive Soviet state which poses the greatest military and economic threat ever to world freedom. Should we do nothing to resolve the factors that have led to our social and economic stagnation? Should we sit idly by as the enslaved citizenry of the Soviet Union begins to out-produce our own free citizenry? Are we a nation that has already reached its peak and is now sliding back? Has something terrible permanently dampened the competitive and idealistic spirit of Americans? Are we destined to live lives of continuously reduced expectations?

Or are we merely resting after two hundred years of solid accomplishments? Perhaps our much discussed complacency will vanish once our citizens are confronted with a policy menu filled with appetizing social, economic, and political choices? Given our current bill of fare, especially the near complete absence of national and community purpose, it is really not so surprising that America is stagnating. Who will deny that our national spirit rarely soars? Who among us does not yearn for something better? Is America ankle deep, knee deep, or chin deep in its self-created pool of quicksand? Whose ears are so clogged that they cannot hear the squeaking apparatus that is our ruined governmental bureaucracy? And who is so blind that he misses the threat to our freedoms that emanates from the policy makers who inhabit our intransigent institutional infrastructure? Who has not felt betrayed by the daily exposures of corruption, bribery, criminality, and wastefulness that flaw our government and those who run it? Who will deny that the vast majority of Americans have almost no voice at all in government, while our well-financed special interest groups dominate national affairs to the detriment of the general interest of all our citizens?

We may turn our backs to it, but in our hearts we know that America seriously lacks the progressive social philosophy and economic prescriptions to change our dismal course as we head toward the twenty-first century. Mere cosmetic surgery is not nearly sufficient to rectify the serious structural flaws afflicting our society and threatening our very superstructure. Even the social progress in hand seems to be slipping away as women and minorities find their hard-won victories easily pierced by neurotic conservatives.

A close examination of just what these so-called staunch pillars of American society are so busily and righteously protecting finds only the sacred distance between the haves and the have-nots, the fortunate and the unfortunate, the vulgar consumers and the needy, the new aristocracy and the modern-day version of the landless serfs.

In the words of the eighteenth century French philosopher Denis Diderot, "We have built a labyrinth and cannot find our way out." Our social, economic, and political headings are askew. Our once vibrant nation is now like an old car on an old road. Both the car and the road have been seriously neglected. The car is rusting out and seems always in need of repair. But, repair one malady and two others immediately crop up. And the road is dangerously full of potholes, and is so aged that it no longer appears on new maps. It is no longer a much traveled road. More than a few have been heard to say that it leads nowhere. On occasion our old car runs on that old road, moving in fits and starts, as has been the case with our recent technical, economic advance, which sometimes appears to be making progress. But appearances often belie reality.

In America, the reality is that one fifth of our entire population—nearly fifty million men, women, and children—live in or near poverty. The already great gap between rich and poor, between privileged and underprivileged, is growing wider with each passing day. Less noted, but still important, is the fact that almost all Americans (only the very wealthy excepted) live their entire lives in a completely unprotected position.

In America we are overgoverned by being undergoverned. The foremost manifestation of this phenomenon is found in that august body, the House of Representatives. That not one in a hundred among us can name even three of the 435 so-called representatives that constitute this legislative body is convincing evidence of the minor role representatives play in the productive aspects of political life. And if you think this somewhat of an overstatement, then conduct for yourself this very simple experiment. Draft your own personal list of the accomplishments of the current 435 House members and their staffs, and include those of their predecessors. These many otherwise honorable men and women in reality do very little to further the general interests of America's citizenry. By law these 435 House members must stand for re-election every two years. Electioneering requires campaign funds, heavy financing. A House member earns $72,600 each year, yet the average member spends $241,500 to get elected, with the most desperate among them spending over $1,000,000.

With such large and frequent requirements for campaign funds is it any wonder that the well financed special interest groups and many House members seem instrinsically linked? And if only because there have been so many of them, the history of the House of Representatives is rife with criminal and ideological corruption. But the failure of House members to produce positive results, and their propensity for the favoritism of special interests is their greatest drawback. What is truly destructive to our democracy is that the House of Representatives epitomizes our intransigent institutional infrastructure.

Every elected official must at times deal with special interest factions. But the fewer the number of officials the easier it is for the citizenry to influence and monitor their activities. The House is now like a large pot of stew to which so many ingredients have been added over such a long period that the original recipe, proportional representation for the more populous states, is no longer discernible nor operative.

What we have instead of that original recipe is a great body of self-seeking self-glorifiers who serve mainly as impediments to social, economic, and political progress in America. The verbal eugenics that so characterize activity in the House of Representatives greatly impede the tempo of experimentation and change in America. And who could be more pleased with this than the neurotic conservative guardians of America's status quo?

There is little hope of transforming America into a truly just society if we continue with a bicameral legislature. America simply does not require such a proliferation of legislators and their equally proliferous staffs on the federal level. Of the twenty-one democracies that have been in existence since the conclusion of World War II, three—New Zealand in 1950, Denmark in 1953, and Sweden in 1970—have shifted from bicameral to unicameral. Not one has shifted to a bicameral legislature. It should be noted with some satisfaction that the three nations that have shifted not only establish a trend for the future composition of democracies but, more importantly, that each of these nations has, since the adoption of unicameralism, greatly accelerated its internal tempo of progressive social, economic, and political experimentation and each has prospered.

If, for the time being, we must continue effectively enchained by the illusion of democracy that emanates from the House of Representatives, then let us rename that body, or at least think of it as, the House of Special Interests.

As we have seen, one of the central aims of **Metacapitalism** is to redirect the federal government's attention from the special interest groups back to the general welfare of American society. Even when segments of our government are poised to serve the general interests of society like the Internal Revenue service (IRS), their potential is thwarted by misbegotten laws, formulated and bastardized by special interest groups who seek to preserve special considerations for themselves. Instead of functioning in a way that severely handicaps the spread of prosperity in America and antagonizes major portions of our population with both direct and indirect intimidations, the IRS should serve as a central clearinghouse for America's transient capital, assuring that the tax laws, as amended by **Metacapitalism's** proposed Prosperity Revenue Act, function to meet the general interests of all Americans.

Metacapitalism represents a significant change of course for American capitalism and American democracy, but one entirely mindful of the social precepts and values motivating the First American Revolution and the creation of our great Constitution. The essential shift in capitalism is away from economic monopolism—the domination of the many by the few—toward programs and policies that restore competition by nurturing an economic environment conducive to the growth of small businesses and farms. The essential shift in democracy is away from the illusions of freedom that have lulled our citizenry into a dangerous complacency. The illusion that we enjoy representative government—equal rights and equal opportunity—is ultimately paralyzing, an image of contentment we have not yet attained.

In the interests of free people the world over, there is no higher priority than for America to recapture its lost momentum. Our past achievements have served as a positive influence. Democracy, itself a relatively new political phenomenon (emerging as it did as late as the eighteenth century), is growing. There are now about fifty-one democratic nations in which dwell some thirty-seven percent of the world's population. There are parliamentary democracies such as Canada, Australia, New Zealand, most of the Nordic nations, most of Western Europe and Japan, where the chief executive of government is selected or appointed by the legislature. And there are the presidential democracies, as in America, Finland, and France, where the chief executive is elected directly by the people. But, though the system of government called democracy is still emerging, like capitalism, all democracies share at least four important features:

1. The inalienable right of each citizen to vote in public elections and to run for public office.

2. Freedom of individual and group expression, including the gathering and dissemination of any and all information not deemed adverse to the interests of national security.

3. Freedom to unite into groups and organizations, such as political parties, unions, religions, corporations, clubs, and other associations.

4. A system of checks and balances to assure the protection and continuance of the above, including strong laws forbidding the advocacy of violence toward fellow citizens and the government.

As the world's first modern democracy (and certainly the first democracy operating under capitalism), America has served admirably as a positive cynosure for both developed and developing nations. We served as active participants in two world wars when the freedom of allied nations was threatened. Even the Soviet leadership uses the American economy as a standard against which its leaders measure the progress of their own society and productivity.

But, as we have seen, much is wrong and much is left undone in America. Those stalwart guardians of our status quo who regularly employ the narrowest of interpretations in constitutional considerations in order to thwart social, economic, and political progress, will bitterly oppose *Metacapitalism's* thirsts and thrusts, particularly its proposal to move from a representative democracy to a citizen-directed democracy. For, once we return the reins of government to the hands of the citizenry, the neurotic conservatives, America's vestigial aristocracy, will head for the hills and stay there.

Citizen-directed democracy is an evolutionary step, just as **Metacapitalism** is an evolution from uncertain capitalism. Though most of the world's democracies are currently representative, most have made good use of the national referendum.

America is the major exception. Our experience of referenda comes primarily from several states, most notably California. There has never been a national referendum in the United States at the federal level. The national referendum is the key to citizen-directed democracy, to expanding upon our existing freedoms, to accelerating the pace of social, economic, and political change in America. The procedural aspects may take a multitude of forms, but for such referenda to be truly useful in the revolutionary sense, they must be citizen-initiated as well as government-initiated. Only by these means can the citizenry control the government and remedy its errors.

The citizen-initiated national referendum will deliver a mortal blow to Soviet tyranny. With it America and the Soviet Union will be politically polar opposites. We shall have on the one hand a truly free people directing their government as they see fit, and, on the other, a truly enslaved people dictated to in even the smallest areas of their daily lives by an inherited, tyrannical government. Yes, inheritance is outlawed in the Soviet Union except for the government, which must be inherited, wanted or not.

METACAPITALISM
AND THE ROCKET'S RED GLARE

The competition between America and the Soviet Union is the contest of free people against slavery, of democracy against totalitarianism, of capitalism against communism. The outcome of this intense and most important competition spells the destiny of mankind for perhaps centuries to come. If freedom, a newcomer to the political arena, is to vanquish totalitarianism, then let it be the very best freedom—real freedom, citizen-directed freedom. Let freedom's victory be complete. Let us not win narrowly, only to find ourselves still enchained by illusions. And let the glow of freedom shine not just on the fortunate, but rather on every person, as we recognize that to comfort and protect the weak among us is the highest task of a free people.

WHY AMERICA LACKS COHERENT ECONOMIC AND INDUSTRIAL POLICIES

There are two voices in America—the voice of the special interest and the voice of the general interest. Special interests are as numerous as the population. Each citizen is a bundle of special interests. Very few of us agree about all the vital issues of our times, much less about local issues and less important national and international issues. A precise count of special interests in America has never been made, but to gain some feel for their magnitude, one need merely to turn to the nineteenth edition of the Encyclopedia of Associations, which lists 18,170 national organizations in the United States dealing with special interest considerations. The vast majority of special interest organizations pose little or no threat to the general interest, that is, to the general interest of the vast majority of Americans. They, like we, are underfinanced, understaffed, and seek limited, quite often important, aims. Both alone and in sum, these special interest organizations demonstrate that freedom is alive and proliferating in America.

There are, however, two distinctive, yet very different, threats to the general interests of all Americans. It is these that thwart America's social, economic, and political advance, and have led to our economic and industrial stagnation.

The first of these leads directly to the second. It is the very real threat posed by a few hundred special interest organizations that have grown so powerful, so well-financed, so strident, so entrenched, so loud, so politically established and connected, that their voices tend to drown out all of the others. And in negating America's other voices, the general interests of all Americans are struck a blow so severe that the voice of the general interest is barely heard anymore. In fact, the general interests of America's citizenry are rarely considered these days. So pitiful is the voice of the general interest when compared to the entrenched special interests that even at election time, our leadership and prospective leaders rarely take cognizance of it, preferring to pander instead to the rich special interest groups who fill their coffers with political contributions. In America today, political power derives far more from a few hundred special interest groups than from the vast majority of the American citizenry. This is a critical trend that *Metacapitalism* seeks to reverse. To reverse it is our only hope for rescuing American capitalism and democracy from the current and pervasive swamp of mediocrity.

What are the general interests of the vast majority of Americans? It is more than interesting, perhaps remarkable, that we should have to ask. From *Metacapitalism's* perspective the more important of the general interests of the American people include:

1. Protecting and expanding upon our birthright freedoms.

2. Protecting our borders and those of other free nations from foreign invasion (this we hear about because it is also of utmost necessity to the powerful special interests).

3. Advancing toward a fuller realization of equal rights and equal opportunity.

4. Nurturing an economic environment to guarantee that all Americans will achieve a degree of financial security, and a retirement with dignity.

5. Nurturing a social environment that posits human rights above property rights, and that aims to sustain those individuals who, for any one of a number of reasons, are not able to sustain themselves adequately in our competitive environment.

6. The protection of the natural environment from unnecessary intrusions, corrosives, and pollutants.

7. The nurture of a political environment that actively seeks a maximum contribution from the people, is thoroughly controlled by the vote of the people, and that encourages the full partici-

pation of the people, particularly their vote on national issues, and their active participation in community affairs.

8. The nurture of a competitive economic environment, replete with a pervasive system of financial and social incentives, and free of economic monopolism.

9. Assuring that every American will have access to medical care when needed, free of financial constraints, and that every qualified student may pursue a higher education on a reasonably competitive basis with every other student, and that the families of students need not mortgage themselves to finance the education of their children.

10. Assuring that the agencies of government, at all levels, pursue policies and programs consistent with the growth in the quality as well as the quantitative aspects of life in America.

These, then, are examples of the general interests of all Americans. There is, however, another national agenda. It is this other agenda that has been dominating us. It is an agenda that pits group against group with an almost imperceptible insidiousness. There are critically important items on this other agenda, items that concern the vast majority of Americans. But a close examination of each of these issues shows that even if finally resolved one way or the other, the class structure, the modern aristocracy, the poverty, the economic insecurity, the great disparities between rich and poor, the economic monopolism, are left untouched. What are the items on this other agenda that has us all so preoccupied that we have all but abandoned active pursuit of our general interests? They are the heated debates over:

1. Whether or not women should have equal rights with men. This issue would be readily resolved in a national referendum and it is quite likely that the equal rights of women would be established for once and for all.

2. Whether or not abortion should be legal, an issue of foremost concern to women, but of concern to men as well. It is hard to forecast the results of a national referendum on this issue but it is likely that the individual choice of the woman would prove victorious.

3. Whether or not there should be capital punishment. Though numerous studies show that capital punishment is no impediment to capital crimes, and may even serve to increase their rate, it is impossible to forecast the outcome of a national referendum on this issue.

4. Whether or not religious prayer should be permitted in public schools. This issue was settled long ago by the Founding Fathers and a national referendum would probably uphold their resolution.

These are but a few of the items on the other agenda that serve to divide Americans, to pit group against group in such a way that attention is almost totally deflected from the general interest of all Americans. *Metacapitalism* contends that our political system, as currently structured, and our current body of economics will never produce policies and programs that get beyond this other agenda to focus on the general interests of the American people. Our body of economic theory and policy is a rather picayune assortment of rationales for tinkering and puttering. Our economists are like the parsimonious driver of an automobile who, ever aware of the cost of gasoline, cautiously applies pressure to the throttle so as to maximize mileage per gallon, without ever questioning the need for the trip itself. Our esteemed economic traditionalists seem quite content with their role as fine-tuners, so content that they do not see the severe flaws that afflict the very foundation of our economy, as well as their economic theories and programs. These contented fine-tuners, products of the entrenched establishment and the guardians of the status quo, replete with institutional biases, will never put forth the bold initiatives required to rescue America from the swamp of mediocrity.

As we have seen, slowly but surely, we have been transformed into a nation of cowering traditionalists, governed by self-seeking, self-glorifying amateurs, who are all but entirely beholden to the guardians of the status quo.

Why do we lack much needed economic and industrial policies? Look around you. Look at our uninvolved, unfeeling, unseeing citizens. Look at the way we vote, for cosmetic solutions and pledges, for slogans and propaganda. When is the last time you spoke up for the general interest? When was the last time you seriously considered personal sacrifice for the general interest? Who among you really wants to restore political, social, and economic vitality to this country? What part are you willing to play? Are you willing to experiment if short-term setbacks mean personal loss and sacrifice? Are you willing to take one step back before taking three steps forward?

Before America can have a coherent economic and industrial strategy sufficient to meet the challenges of the twenty-first century, Americans themselves must gain a greater understanding of the evolutionary possibilities for democracy and capitalism, and begin to see them not as fixed ideological categories, but rather as man-made political and economic systems that will evidence positive growth only to the extent that they are positively influenced by man.

DOES AMERICA WANT OR NEED COHERENT ECONOMIC AND INDUSTRIAL POLICIES?

As we approach the twenty-first century, we find that life in America is dominated by a highly complex system of all but invisible dependencies. As we have seen, most Americans are far removed from the ownership of productive resources, the classical means of production, except for their individual labor. Even the family unit, which could once be counted on for complementary productive efforts, has been effectively dismantled. Very few Americans are in any sort of position to fend for themselves, even as regards the basic requirements of life—food, clothing, and shelter. Instead, we depend upon one, another for the application of individual skills which together produce a vast assortment of goods and services.

This invisible system of interdependencies has been relatively stable, at least since the Great Depression. Now most Americans are too young to have any direct memory of that event, and even for those who lived through it, the stark terrors that ensued from the massive societal deprivation have all but faded from memory. Certainly we have experienced repeated economic ups and downs, the ups called booms, the downs called recessions. In fact, our most recent recession bore several of the characteristics that marked the Great Depression. There was massive unemployment (variously estimated at fifteen to thirty million), the banking system verged on failure (and is still in a highly precarious situation), and real family income dropped (and has not risen for twenty-five years). Fortunately, the recession was reversed by massive government spending before it grew into a full-fledged depression. Yet, the immediate specter of depression was upon us. If it had struck, the devastation that would have been wrought today would make the Great Depression of the 1930s seem mild.

Today, America's advanced industrial economy is far more complex in its numerous interrelationships than it was in the 1920s, 1930s, and 1940s. An incident or event at one point on our economic network will have an all but immediate impact on other points on the network. When a major commercial bank verges on collapse, as several have recently, our entire economy is placed in jeopardy. Today, more highly leveraged speculative instruments and markets exist than were ever dreamed of in those earlier decades. Recently, two brothers tried to corner the silver market by speculating massively with silver futures and the resulting defaults almost brought the entire financial industry to its knees. And this is no isolated event. Each year the national news is filled with instances of enormous financial improprieties, mismanagement, overspec-

113

ulation and the like. In Boston recently, several banks have been caught up in the illegal laundering of money and have pleaded guilty to felony charges. Many of the nation's largest banks teeter on the edge of bankruptcy because they have imprudently exported our nation's working capital in the form of commercial loans, often at usurious rates, to developing nations who simply cannot maintain the long-term economic momentum to repay them. The state banking system in Ohio recently fell into serious trouble, was temporarily shut down, leaving depositors trembling, and was finally rescued by the Federal Reserve Bank. In times of crisis the states, as well as the corporate monopolies, turn immediately to the federal government for assistance. When times are normal, these same entities preach federalism and corporate isolationism so that they may be free to pursue their own selfish interests which more often than not are highly exploitative of the majority of Americans and work against the general interests of us all.

In 1930 there were only 122.8 million of us; since then our population has almost doubled. In 1930 there were 6.3 million farms; today there are fewer than 3 million. Who will feed the nearly 250 million of us if these remaining farms begin to fail? In 1930 so few people received any form of transfer payment from the federal government that no one bothered keeping statistics. Today, nearly every man, woman, and child is covered by Social Security and receives some form of direct or indirect transfer payment from the federal government (tax deductions are nothing but disguised federal subsidies).

What will happen to our fellow citizens if these payments or coverages are cut? Social Security is the primary retirement plan for a majority of Americans. It is not a dole. Most of them spent decades paying into the Social Security Fund. But, does it provide enough for a dignified retirement? You know the answer. In 1930 our Gross National Product was less than one-tenth of the nearly $4 trillion it is in 1985. Given our vast population growth, our great distance from the means of production, the leveraged nature and complexity of our financial markets, our virtual dependence on transfer payments from the federal government, what will happen if a severe recession or depression strikes? What will happen is that each of us, the rich and the poor, the employed and the unemployed, the old and the young, the innocent and the guilty, the active and the passive, will experience horror and terror the likes of which are usually reserved for war.

The American economy has reached its most critical threshold. In a few short years, if (given our current economic and social policies) we are fortunate enough to avoid another Great Depression, our annual output of goods and services will have grown to $6 trillion, approximately $24,000 per capita. The Soviets have protected themselves from the vicissitudes of international markets by implementing a policy of economic isolation. In a free society such a policy is neither feasible nor desirable. Ours is supposedly a market, not a managed economy. But that does not mean that we must sit idly by awaiting what the future will bring. That does not mean that nothing can be done. That does not mean that we must continue along the path of excessive economic timidity, attempting to manage unemployment, tinkering with interest rates and the money supply as our only recourse to economic action.

Over the last five years there have appeared from a variety of sources a number of proposals for an American industrial policy. The most published and discussed of these proposals takes the form of having the federal government immerse itself in private industry by somehow selecting those industries that are destined to prosper, providing them with financial incentives in the form of tax benefits or government loans, while those industries that are destined to be losers would be gradually phased out of existence. Just who and how anyone would go about the selection process was not often discussed and ultimately proved to be the fatal flaw inherent in all such proposals. We must never yield to the temptation to insinuate the federal government directly into the private business sector of our economy.

There are two fundamental reasons for steadfastly maintaining a strict division between our public and private sectors. First, the decision-making that governs production and distribution in our economy is highly decentralized, distributed in various degrees to every producer and consumer in our society (and that includes just about everyone). The participation of nearly every person in deciding what and how much to produce is far more productive than any centralized planning system could ever be, both in terms of overall efficiency and the variety of goods and services produced. Even more important is

116

the multifaceted freedom inherent in our decentralized and distributed decision making processes, freedom to pursue the employment or career of one's choice, to start a business, to innovate, to energize, and many others. These market freedoms enable us to pursue highly personal objectives and life styles in almost unlimited diversity. And it is this very energized diversity that serves to distinguish capitalism from communism, that enriches the tapestry of life in democracy as opposed to the drabness that characterizes totalitarian societies. Only those who have directly experienced the horrors of entrapment, imprisonment, or slavery can know fully that one month of freedom is worth more than a year under totalitarianism.

Yet, given our uncertain capitalism, the federal government is already far too active in the private sector of our economy and instead of advancing economic development it serves as one of the greatest barriers to long-term economic prosperity. It is already the primary source of sustenance of a multitude of special interests that thwart competition and are the epitome of economic monopolism. We must begin to restructure the economic role of the federal government, recognizing that its only legitimate private sector role is that which must be done to advance or protect the general interest, which is the interest of all Americans: the protection of consumers and the environment against corrosive or corrupt elements and of our citizenry from discriminatory practices and the like. No other intrusions in the microeconomy, like rescuing the giant banks and corporations should be tolerated.

METACAPITALISM
AND THE ROCKET'S RED GLARE

America's approach toward establishing viable economic and industrial strategy for economic development and the spread of prosperity as we approach life in the twenty-first century must avoid both the totalitarianism that has effectively enslaved the Soviet citizenry and produced a brutish and utterly drab society, and the special interest orientation that dominates the grab bag of our current social programs or those of countries with relatively static, homogeneous populations. Instead of merely stretching to reach a higher level, America must break out of the swamp of mediocrity in which we are drowning. We must set our social, economic, and political objectives high, higher than we have heretofore thought possible. A comprehensive economic and industrial policy at the macro level of our economy, one that serves to expand both competition and industrial productivity is within our power. But to achieve it we must truly strive to cast aside our excessive timidity, and experiment. We must be ready to absorb those sacrifices that always attend social, economic, and political experimentation.

Historically, we are a nation of people in transition, of people seeking a better life in a new land. This seeking of a better life has been a historical strength in our nation's development, and it must continue to prove our strength. Historically, we are also a nation of individualists, perhaps not so much the rugged adventurers that pioneered our frontiers, but certainly economic individualists. We are a land of millions upon millions of small businesses and farms without which we are unrecognizable as America. Yet, even this, possibly our greatest industrial asset, is threatened by the invidious onslaught of economic monopolism.

Since the first decades of the Industrial Revolution our economy has experienced transformations ranging from the revolution in labor to the electronic and bio-chemical revolutions. For the most part, the frontier capi-talist, the captain of industry, has vanished from our economic scene, replaced by veritable armies of career-oriented executives, employed by the giant corporations to advance the cause of economic monopolism. In terms of economic might and political clout, the few sit on top and crush the many. America's industrial elite is but two to five hundred corporations at the first tier, followed by another one thousand to two thousand corporations at the second tier, tens of thousands at the third tier, and finally by millions of small businesses and farms at the fourth tier.

For the most part, it is the first tier corporations, which employ only a small percentage of America's workforce, and are far less profitable than small busi-nesses, that tend to impede social justice and the spread of economic prosperity. It is here that the desperate pur-suit of even increasing gains in sales and profitability leads to economic monopolism, the subsequent destruc-tion of viable competition, the withholding of new tech-nology and new products, environmental pollution, bumbling inefficiency, dehumanizing employment prac-tices, corruption and political chicanery. The first tier con-tinuously threatens the other tiers, as well as the general interest of all Americans, with a vast arsenal of guises, intimidations and outright coercion. In all of nature, at least in so far as has been yet determined, every species has both an optimum and maximum size. And the various prehistoric species that evolved into behemoths also managed to evolve out of existence. The giant corporations of today seem altogether akin to the prehistoric behemoths in that they threaten both their environment and themselves with extinction.

Economic monopolism serves only the narrowest interests and never the long-term general interest. Monopolism, as we see it today, results not so much from a fundamental flaw in the theory or practice of capitalism, but rather from a misguided or confused notion of what constitutes economic monopolism, inattention to established antitrust laws, and the way the vestigal aristocracy that still manages to fashion an elitist base. As categories of human action capitalism and democracy and the wedding of the two are still evolving.

One of America's foremost strengths, though one which is usually overlooked, is that even given the hostile encroachments of the monopolies, we remain essentially a nation of small businesses and farmers. Not once has a small business upset an entire community by repairing to another location. Not once has a small business severely jeopardized the financial superstructure of our economy. And it is not the small farms but rather the farming monopolies that lobby for artificial price supports and special government subsidies. The economic monopolies have served to retard progress in America. They also serve to afflict us with an ungainly assortment of inferior products. The inferiority of product that emanates from willful policies of planned obsolescence is part and parcel of the giant corporations continuous pursuit of even increasing sales. In almost every industry in America, if it is quality of product or innovation that you seek, you will find it in the small businesses and not in the large. Thus, an American economic and industrial policy must build upon our given strengths and seek to add to them. Economic monopolism only appears to be a strength, an appalling misperception which must not mislead us.

Ultimately, the decision as to whether or not America will have a viable economic and industrial policy becomes political. If there is to be a transcendence from uncertain capitalism to *Metacapitalism's* also ultimately a political decision. Nothing but more of the same, over and over again, is likely to happen until an inspired and emboldened American citizenry demands that it happens. In a phrase, it is highly unlikely that the stalwart guardians of the status quo will precipitate revolutionary social, economic, and political change. This much has certainly been proved. But a now apathetic citizenry suddenly turned passionate can work wonders. For example, working within the existing system of law, woefully inadequate as it is, a majority of America's citizens could bring *Metacapitalism's* social, economic, and political program into existence. The primary hindrance lies in the way we vote, which is for representatives rather than directly on the issues. By keeping the American people away from direct voting, the founding fathers evidenced a deep-seated distrust for majority rule. Considering the systems of government from which they had fled, that they were motivated to representational democracy was then highly revolutionary, a keen blow to authoritarianism. Under authoritarian or totalitarian regimes, those in power seek to protect what they have, which is usually almost everything. This led to democracy which itself has now in America been captured by a coalition of ruling interests which heretofore we have labeled the neurotic conservatives. They, like the aristocracies of old, seek to protect that which they have, which also like the aristocracies of old is almost every thing. As we have seen, their willful special interest oriented actions consign the majority of Americans to lives of economic insecurity, and many others to lives of utter desperation.

What follows is **Metacapitalism's** program for a Second American Revolution. Its twelve legislative initiatives may be viewed as an update to our historic Bill of Rights. These initiatives assume that a vast majority of Americans wish for themselves, for their fellow citizens, and for the world at large a better life, a life filled with more than fleeting moments of happiness, a life of expanding rather than contracting freedoms, a life with dignity and expanded opportunities, a life of participation and caring, freed from the oppressions which now alienate a great portion of our citizenry, a more secure life, a life based on principles of fairness and a witness to real social justice.

Some of us question whether or not such a life is possible. Some, mostly the neurotic conservatives, tell us it is not and that even if it were it would not be desirable.

From **Metacapitalism's** perspective the time to debate is behind us. We must move now or never. Soviet aggression, both ideological and economic, is bearing down upon us. Its nature is relentless. American capitalism and American democracy must be modernized or run the risk of failure.

Part IV

METACAPITALISM'S SOCIAL,
ECONOMIC, AND POLITICAL
PROGRAM FOR A SECOND
AMERICAN REVOLUTION

A SECOND AMERICAN REVOLUTION INTRODUCED

The vast majority of Americans have been effectively degraded and enslaved by the economic myths and mischief that fashion the American economy, and have made the idea of capitalism itself uncertain. American white and blue collar workers, farmers, executives, and proprietors, all are chained to their occupations, with little opportunity for economic security, or to change the conditions that oppress and abuse them, and improve the quality of their lives and those of their fellow citizens. Since the creation of our remarkable Constitution, the small handful of people who possess the entirety of our nation's wealth have purposely built a seemingly indestructible barrier between American politics (democracy) and American economics (capitalism). Political issues, and the public sector, are addressed by government. Economic issues are relegated to the private sector where the economic monopolists reign supreme and dictate the course of economic development and the current and future distribution of national income and wealth. This separation of the political from the economic is arbitrary and serves only to insure the continuing enslavement of a vast majority of Americans by possessors of mostly unearned wealth, the guardians of the status quo, and their numerous agents. America's citizenry is enslaved by the retrogressive interests of the economic monopolists, while the citizens of the Soviet Union are enslaved by the repressive acts of the Soviet State.

In the Soviet Union the entire citizenry is employed by the State, which, as we have seen, owns the entire productive apparatus; land, mineral resources, capital, machinery. Without state sponsorship, a Soviet citizen is reduced to beggary or starvation. State ownership and control of the economy are used to intimidate and coerce people into complying with State policies and practices. Failure to conform leads directly to economic punishment, social harassment, and finally to imprisonment, exile, and death.

For most people in America, neither economic or political conditions are as harsh as in the Soviet Union. Americans may vote, speak their minds, publish, travel, pray, and enjoy a variety of other personal freedoms not permitted under Soviet totalitarianism. However, many in America do not have full access of their freedoms because of their economic enslavement, and even moderate nonconformism produces social ostracization and economic deterioration. Our freedom to vote is constrained by our representatives; usually political amateurs who are the direct or indirect agents of the economic monopolists. We have never had the freedom of opportunity to vote on national issues. Such a freedom would surely pose a great threat to the economic monopolists. Only the direct vote on issues, within the context of a citizen-initiated legislative agenda, as described in *Metacapitalism's* Voting Powers Act, will deliver the American economy and economic prosperity to the American people.

In economic life, as with voting, there is also an illusion of freedom. Americans are free to choose how they will earn a living, restrained only by ambition, mental capacity, and the fulfillment of necessary educational, vocational, or other preparatory requirements. That the children of the wealthy are royalty in comparison to the children of the poor, that their unearned money produces a distinct and often decisive competitive edge, is ignored in the vast majority of political propaganda that espouses the glories of so-called American equal rights and equal opportunity.

In America, nearly the entire productive apparatus is either owned or controlled by less than five percent of the citizenry, and this concentration of economic power grows with each passing day. An enormous percentage of America's working population is effectively controlled by the economic monopolists, while the remainder is self-employed or works for government. These actual percentages vary greatly based on definitional perspectives of employment and economic control, but from *Metacapitalism's* perspective the lot of the American worker under the economic monopolists is every bit as grievous as the lot of the Soviet worker under the state.

The American worker, while entitled to greater personal freedoms than Soviet workers, has far less economic security. American workers may have larger incomes, but nothing but a pittance of an unemployment insurance and welfare—a truly obnoxious system—stands between the American worker and his family and starvation.

The Social Security Act of 1935 (SSA) was government's first major assault on the economic power of the economic monopolists, one over which they are still angry and still aggressively working to overthrow. Considering the obstacles that the monopolists had placed in its path, it is remarkable that even this mediocre penetration of private sector economic control by public sector policy was possible. SSA marked the first recognition by government that the separation between political and economic issues had grown too wide and had brought the nation to the brink of a worker revolution. Were it not for the fact that the Great Depression was driving even entrenched wealth to distraction with the fear that they would lose all that they had, not even the quite visible human horrors of the day would have moved the government to act. Finally, after years of inaction under President Herbert Hoover, then newly elected President Franklin Delano Roosevelt, following the economic prescriptions of British Lord John Maynard Keynes, began to prime the pump, forcing government to spend money it had not raised, the beginning of what is today referred to as the federal deficit. The Keynesian medicine proved altogether appropriate. The American and world economies began to rebound from the depths of depression, and in this atmosphere of jubilant recovery, the monopolists were too busy counting their recaptured fortunes to work against passage of the

Social Security Act of 1935. But they have recovered. At the time, SSA seemed a suitable beginning for the evolution of governmental accountability and responsibility for the economic security of the American people. In retrospect, Social Security is not sufficient to place a retiree beyond poverty, much less to provide workers retirement with dignity.

Since World War II, the monopolists have been busily reconstructing the wall between politics and economics. As we have seen, the Full Employment Act was purely cosmetic, and is now rotting in the basement of the Congress. Each new economic contraction and particularly the deeper recessions demonstrate beyond all doubt the financially precarious position of the majority of Americans. Even in what are called prosperous times, twenty to thirty million Americans (forty percent of them children) live in poverty. The monopolists force American workers to survive without access to the means of production. A lifetime's work is obliterated or a geographical area economically devastated by the summary actions of employers against employees. Our rapidly advancing technology has led to an advanced industrial economy in constant transition with regard to the prerequisites for new employment. Dismissed workers are often left high and dry, without suitable alternative employment, or without employment prospects of any kind. A full half century since passage of the Social Security Act finds the vast majority of Americans economically insecure, both at work and in retirement. As for the Full Employment Act of 1946, not much need be said beyond the fact that it has been reduced to a virtual sham. The stalwart guardians of the status quo have labored intently and successfully on strengthening their self-serving wall between political issues and economic issues. It is one of *Metacapitalism's* most urgent tasks to upset their retrogressive aims by removing that wall in a way that capitalizes on American strengths and avoids the twin traps of 'state' economic totalitarianism, as under Soviet communism, or 'state' economic authoritarianism, as under French socialism. In sum, it seeks to replace representative democracy with citizen-directed democracy, as outlined in the Voting Powers and Political Reform Acts, and to rout economic monopolism with strategies, programs, and policies that promote small enterprise by passage of Prosperity Revenue, National Capital, Corporate Reform, and Financial Reform Acts. It has not been the monopolists, but rather the daily toil and ingenuity of many millions of men and women that has opened our vast land to the promise of equal rights and equal opportunity. And it would be a disgrace to civilization to stop here, or to regress. America verges on becoming a truly great and compassionate society. For the sake of all humanity, we must complete the task.

The transition from uncertain capitalism may take a year, or it may take several generations. It will take far more than the twelve legislative initiatives that are proposed as *Metacapitalism.* There must be a revolution in the body of economic theory that today guides government economic policy making. This revolution is approaching, but at a snail's pace. Each day a new book or article attacks the conceptual foundations of the mixed bag of macroeconomic and microeconomic theory that underlies the thinking behind American economic policy. Much of the blame for this must be placed on the establishment economists, whose excessive timidity has kept them locked onto a course that they know is wrong. In their eagerness to establish economics as a science, on an academic footing with mathematics, physics, chemistry, and biology, economists have gone to great pains to transfigure what are in fact no more than *a posteriori* observations into *a priori* postulations or natural laws. On top of this they have built elaborate mathematical models of the economy that incorporate the various elements of the so-called natural laws they have unearthed, only to find that the hoped-for capabilities for prediction did not emerge. The majority of free world economists act more like agents of the economic monopolists than like independent thinkers, and treat the subject matter of economics as if it were a closed system like mathematics of physics. In truly closed systems there are constant relationships so strong that other elements that crop up may be dismissed as irrelevant. These strong relationships allow scientists to predict future behavior, such as the orbits of the planets, chemical interactions, and genetic dispositions, with great accuracy. But employment rates, inflation, the money supply, interest rates, markets, investment, forms of capital, supply and demand, are not physical things impelled by the discoverable universal laws, but rather episodic events and objects emanating from political and social structures. Economics and politics are not closed systems; they are open, flexible systems created by people. The supposed laws that govern human economic and political events are in reality not laws at all, but rather abstract generalizations of human behavior. There is no natural rate of interest, no optimum rate of economic growth, no natural rate of unemployment, no natural rate of investment, no natural or predictable pattern of business cycles, no natural distribution of income and wealth. What has been created by people can be re-created by people. A national economic policy that greatly favors economic monopolism, as in America, can readily be changed to favor small enterprise. Nothing like gravity or even inertia impedes the spread of economic security in America—merely the economic, social, and political policies and programs of the entrenched status quo.

The mere existence of the Soviet Union and the Scandinavian bloc of nations with their vastly differing social, economic, and political systems proves that the laws governing these systems are created by people and not by nature. The harsh American market economy, the savage Soviet managed economy, and the benevolent Scandinavian mixed economies are all creations within the context of political and social structures. Change the politics, change the social structure, and you change the economics.

Soviet totalitarian communism's economic system sanctions massive state control over Soviet citizens, subordinating individual freedoms for the sake of the so-called 'common good,' a good entirely determined by the Supreme Soviet without consultation of the citizenry. The

Soviet economic system is a central dictatorship that has grossly abused and enslaved its citizenry in the name of economic development. On the other side America's uncertain capitalism tends to emphasize and glorify those freedoms emanating from private property and private ownership of the productive apparatus. As we have seen, this elevation of material over human conditions has fostered much societal inequity and injustice. Who has seen a contract drawn to favor the poor or the disenfranchised? An unfettered market economy is a Darwinian jungle where only the fittest thrive. Taken to its furthest extreme, an unchecked market economy will yield but a single firm, and that firm will wield powers not unlike those seen in the Soviet Union.

Human intervention is required to correct human error. We must not sit idly by as our system acquires the regressive characteristics of the Soviet economic system. We must opt, instead, for continued social, economic, and political evolution of the sort encapsulated in **Metacapitalism.**

THE VOTING POWERS ACT (VPA)

The Voting Powers Act is a key piece of legislation for the expansion of freedom within an established democracy and for the evolution of uncertain capitalism into **Metacapitalism.** It will turn the incomplete democracy of the United States into a fully mobilized and active democratic system, where each citizen takes his or her full place in the government of the country. The enfranchisement of the American electorate to vote directly on issues of national concern, rather than relying on the actions of their elected representatives is a top priority of **Metacapitalism.**

Background

American democracy is a representative system, whereby the nation governs itself by the free election of representatives. Abraham Lincoln's idea of democracy, which has profoundly affected the political life of America, was that democratic government conforms closely to what the majority of citizens deems desirable in any given situation. The argument could be made, however, that all a representative democracy proves is that the electorate is free on the day of the elections. As soon as political power is placed at one remove from the people, they lose control of their own fate.

In America today the notion of full democracy is further fragmented by the fact that a vast segment of the electorate declines to vote. This voter boycott reflects the alienation of citizens, the conviction that a single vote is meaningless, and that it will be ignored by the nation's representatives. This feeling of impotence prevents vast numbers of voters from exercising the first of those basic freedoms won in the American Revolution—a second revolution is needed to return to them that right.

Today it cannot be said that in America democracy is by or for the people. The people's conception of itself in relation to government paralyzes the individual and collective will. Added to that, the unresponsiveness of government to the articulated opinions of vocal majorities, as in the case of the support of the Equal Rights Amendment, conspires with voter timidity to constrict the scope of individual freedoms and the humanitarian evolution of democracy and capitalism.

There are approximately fifty-two democratic nations in the world today, twenty-one of which have been functioning continuously since World War II. Of the twenty-one established democracies, only America has never held a national referendum. Of those democracies which use referenda, Switzerland has used it most frequently. The national referendum is often used to decide on major financial and constitutional issues. Great Britain went to the polls to decide whether or not it should enter the Common Market (passed), and whether the central government should devolve some of its powers to Scotland and Wales (rejected).

There are two types of national referendum: the one government initiated (which is by far the dominant); the other citizen-initiated (more revolutionary by far, and so far used only in Switzerland and Italy). The national referendum is greatly feared by the stalwart guardians of America's status quo. In both theory and practice it is intended to speed the tempo of social, economic, and political change. The national referendum is particularly conducive to the achievement of constitutional change. The implementation of *Metacapitalism's* legislative agenda within a reasonable time frame would be greatly enhanced by citizen-initiated national referenda.

Objectives

VPA is crucial to the project of enacting *Metacapitalism's* legislative agenda. Only by empowering the people to vote directly on national issues will the vicelike grip of America's vestigial aristocracy be loosened. The special interest orientation of America's elected representatives, regardless of their public ideological claims, is a permanent obstacle to the achievement of social justice.

VPA will help develop a greater general interest orientation among the electorate; voter apathy and alienation will be significantly reduced because citizens will become more involved in national issues, more knowledgeable about America's future legislative options, more demanding of responsiveness from elected representatives, and more eager to participate in local and community affairs. VPA will unlock the stranglehold of the entrenched, elitist guardians of the status quo, unlock our institutional infrastructure, and provide a positive cynosure of real democracy emerging from illusory democracy, of original freedoms nurturing expanded freedoms.

Obstacles

There are no concrete obstacles to the establishment of a process of national referenda in America. Such referenda have already been used at the state level. Twenty-six states have adopted procedures for their use, the earliest in South Dakota in 1898, and the most recent in Florida in 1972. The state referendum was used in Oregon in 1910 to abolish the invidious poll tax, and then again in 1912 to introduce woman's suffrage. Recently, Michigan and Maine prohibited the sale of disposable soft drink containers by popular vote referenda, and Colorado voters rejected the use of their state for the Olympics. In New Jersey it was a referendum that established the legitimacy of casino gambling. But only Arizona, California, Colorado, North Dakota, Oregon, and Washington use them to any significant degree today.

There is active resistance to adopting such a revolutionary and liberating approach to citizen-directed government. In 1978 Senator James Abourzek brought a national initiative and referendum proposal before the Senate (Senate Joint Resolution 67), but the proposal was never brought to a vote. Even proposed amendments to the Constitution are the product of the votes of state legislatures, rather than the direct vote of the people.

It could be argued that the reason Switzerland can hold such frequent referenda lies partly in the smallness of the country. The sheer size and geographical dispersion of America's electorate could, in earlier days, be cited as significant impediments to a national referendum process. Now, the revolutions in electronics and communications make these procedural objections absurd.

By far the greatest remaining obstacles to national referenda in America are the elite's fear of government by and for the people, and the pervasive apathy that already afflicts vast segments of America's electorate.

Discussion

There are those who, appealing to fear, will argue that the issues of our times are too complex for the popular vote, that demagoguery will prevail, that the electorate will become confused, the process indiffident. But the facts of the referendum process show otherwise.

The European experience with such referenda has produced nothing that could be construed as either demagogical or obstructionist. In fact, it is only by becoming politically *active* that a community can become politically sophisticated. The process of civic education broadens the perceptions, rather than deadening them.

There is no party political bias inherent in the referendum procedure. In the twenty-six American states that have used it, both liberal and conservative causes have been advanced. Presented with the full information about the choices available to them, voters will be able to make mature, informed decisions. In Massachusetts voters are provided with voter information packets which contain summaries of each proposal, majority and minority views, and the statements of both proponents and opponents. Such information packets could easily be made nationally available during a referendum.

Conclusion

It is difficult to conceive anything more consistent with and more favorable and natural to the evolution of democracy than a progression from representational democracy to citizen-directed democracy. A Voting Powers Act will hasten the transformation of America into a just society and provide the much needed mechanism for the translation of **Metacapitalism** from theory into practice. In the words of President Franklin Delano Roosevelt, "We have nothing to fear but fear itself."

141

THE PROSPERITY REVENUE ACT (PRA)

Much that is amiss in America today—our stagnating democracy and our stagnating capitalism—results from our atrocious taxation systems, particularly our federal taxation system. This abomination has been called a system "spawned by Karl Marx," by President Ronald Reagan, and "a disgrace to the human race," by President Jimmy Carter. In fact, almost every American agrees that our current federal tax code meets none of the various tests that make for a decent or tolerable system. It is neither fair, equitable, simple, nor efficient. It strangles economic development rather than promoting it. Its elitest bias favors wealth and property over income and people and is more than anachronistic—it is repugnant.

It is nothing less than miraculous that American capitalism has performed as well as it has, given the inhibiting characteristics of the current federal tax law. The unbelievable complexity of the voluminous tax code conceals an abundance of ill-conceived principles, misbegotten policies, misshaped laws, and imbalanced practices. And this is no accident. America's federal system of taxation fails by design. It taxes only income and ignores wealth. In an advanced industrial society it is absurd to consider any tax system as fair as long as it intentionally ignores taxing individual and corporate wealth.

In America, today, some $10 trillion to $20 trillion of entrenched wealth is purposely left untaxed, while almost every form of income is taxed, taxed, and taxed again. Middle income earners are consistently despoiled. Fed the myth of the progressive income tax—that the rich supposedly pay a higher tax rates—they end up behind the eight ball because tax loopholes and preferences specifically designed to favor the rich reduce their actual tax rates to less than those of low and middle income earners. And if that isn't grievance enough, tax monies are confiscated by their employers for transfer to the government. Such confiscatory tax practices are ample evidence that the rich and powerful mistrust the majority of Americans— they fear a taxpayer revolt, which would result in government receiving substantially less money than at present.

The current system of federal taxation is grossly unfair and unproductive, as are the three alternative proposals presently being considered by the Congress—the Reagan-Regan, Kemp-Kasten, and Bradley-Gephardt measures. All Americans end up as losers because these systems serve to retard economic development. Poor and middle income groups end up the biggest losers because only income, and not wealth, is taxed. Many Americans who have toiled throughout their adult years find impoverishment rather than peaceful retirement in their closing years. Many who might otherwise be productive spend inordinate amounts of time counting and protecting their money. Many of them live entirely useless lives and are so inhuman that gazing upon those most unfortunate and in need doesn't produce a whit of a benevolent response. Only trivial consumption and neurotic dependencies fill their empty hours, a form of societal alienation that has enriched many a psychological therapist.

PRA seeks to transform the notion and practice of taxation from that of bitter medicine to that of a healthful serum; one that protects society from the ravages of economic cycles and uncertainties and advances the general interest by promoting economic development and the spread of economic prosperity.

Background

A government without means of financial support will not long maintain its ability to attend to the affairs of society. To finance its activities, a government may exercise several options. In antiquity it was common practice to invade neighboring villages and tribes, confiscating their wealth and enslaving their people. The Greek and Roman Empires expanded this concept to include entire countries and geographical regions. The quest for spoils to finance government runs the full political-historical spectrum, and hardly a major nation in existence today is free from guilt.

Governmental plundering may be wrapped in a variety of cloaks, such as religious zealotry (the Crusades from the end of the eleventh century to the end of the thirteenth), or border integrity (such as the Soviet invasions of Afghanistan, Poland, Hungary, and Czechoslovakia). But, at bottom, incursions are almost always motivated by a government's need for funds, though in the case of the Soviet Union such motivations are well-disguised.

The quest for profits in the international arena today is not so different from the quest for plunder in the past. America's uncertain capitalism invades other nations not with tanks, but with an unseemly exploitative attitude. Nothing better reflects the extent of this commercial invasion than our commercial banking interests, who have brought more than a handful of underdeveloped and developing nations to the verge of international bankruptcy. The insecurity that reigns in the Soviet Union motivates their military aggression; at the same time a stagnating American capitalism is caught *in flagrante delicto*, extracting usurious interest from the very nations it claims to be assisting. Much of the world is thus caught, victimized, by the conflicting, but aggressive, ideologies of the two super-powers.

But the days of empire and exploitation are waning. Governments must fund themselves from within their own borders, and do it in such a way as to encourage economic prosperity rather than retard it. Just after our revolution, the government of the Confederation of States was more a league of gentlemen bound by oath to a spirit of co-operation than a working central government. There was a small army, consisting of about eight hundred men, no executive, and no judiciary. At one point in the 1780s, when the Congress requested $10 million from the states to pay its debts, it ended up with less than twenty percent of that sum, with one state refusing to pay any part of the federal debt.

Today, our government employs twenty times more people than inhabited the whole country in the days just following the American Revolution. With our GNP nearing an annual rate of $4 trillion and a population nearing 250 million, our nation has reached a critical point. By almost every social standard ever seriously used, we appear to be an extremely rich nation, with per capita income running to approximately $16 thousand per annum.

Yet, as we have seen, many severe social, and economic problems persist. Wages are stagnant. The gap between rich and poor is widening. Economic insecurity is pervasive. Economic monopolism is rampant. Small farms are disappearing. Approximately twenty million children live in or near poverty. The cost of education and medical care has soared. In sum, the American Dream has been stopped in its tracks. But, just as the Voting Powers Act with its citizen-initiated national referenda will bring a new vitality to America's democracy, a thorough reformation of our system of federal taxation will help rout the economic stagnation that has beset American capitalism.

Just how ridiculously complicated current federal tax law is was more than adequately demonstrated by the results of one experiment. A very simple test case was devised, using a fictional couple with one child. Assistance in preparing their federal tax return was obtained from twenty-two separate offices of the Internal Revenue Service. Each office calculated a different tax, with results ranging from a liability of $52 to a refund due of $812.

But such unnecessary complexity is not the worst of it. Well beyond the grotesque, verging on pure evil, is the vast array of tax preferences and tax loopholes that serve to transform what is purported to be a progressive tax system into a regressive tax system. A study conducted by the government's own Office of Management and the Budget shows that in just a single year, in the early 1980s, preferences and loopholes reduced the general tax revenue by nearly $300 billion. And these are only the tip of the iceberg. In 1984 America's GNP was nearly $4 trillion. From this the federal government collected approximately $700 billion, ninety-one percent of which came from the personal income tax, social insurance taxes, and the corporate income tax. The personal income tax accounted for $308 billion, social insurance taxes for $263 billion, and corporate income taxes were $70 billion, with the remaining nine percent coming from a variety of sources, such as federal excise taxes ($38 billion), estate and gift taxes ($6 billion), customs duties ($9 billion), and the remainder from a number of miscellaneous fees and taxes. Thus, by direct tax on their profits, corporations paid only ten percent of total federal receipts in 1984. Even worse, many highly profitable corporations paid nothing at all. A recent study by the Citizens for Tax Justice found that more than half of the nation's 250 most profitable corporations paid not one sou in federal income tax. The General Electric Corporation had $6.5 billion in domestic pretax profits for 1981 to 1983 and paid nothing, while claiming $283 million in tax refunds for prior years. At least six other companies, including Boeing, Dow Chemical, Tenneco, Santa Fe Southern Pacific, Weyerhauser and Du Pont, claimed refunds in excess of $100 million, though their combined profits were in excess of $10 billion. General Dynamics has paid virtually no federal taxes since 1972, taking full advantage of a tax loophole called "completed contract" accounting.

The giant corporations were not alone in avoiding or evading their federal tax responsibilities. In 1981, 226 American families with incomes in excess of $200,000 paid not a cent in federal taxes. And the Brookings Institute reports that the actual federal income tax rate for people earning over $1 million a year is 17.7 percent, less than the rate for many middle income families.

The federal government now spends over $50 billion a year in pursuit of less than $350 billion in individual and corporate income taxes. And on top of this incredible waste is stacked another $50 to $100 billion spent in unproductive time and dollars to record expenses and prepare tax returns. The preparation of tax returns is so complicated an undertaking that more than forty million individuals and more than fifteen million businesses seek the assistance of professional tax accountants and lawyers, whose fees, ironically, are deductible. Why so much? Consider these numbers. Each year approximately

100 million tax returns are prepared, 80 million by individuals and 20 million by businesses. The Federal Tax Code itself numbers over 200 volumes and weighs in excess of 300 pounds. In 1981, the Federal Tax Form 1040, the one used by the majority of individual Americans, was seventeen pages long and contained an additional forty-four pages of instructions.

Of late, instigated by President Ronald Reagan's enthusiastic support for it, there has been much ado over tax reform. The current administration has fashioned a modified flat tax proposal, often referred to as the Reagan-Regan plan, which varies from, but incorporates many of the features of two previous modified flat tax proposals, the Bradley-Gephart, and Kemp-Kasten bills. The major surface similarities of the three so-called tax reform plans is that each lowers and reduces the number of tax rates, and each eliminates certain deductible expenses.

Beneath the surface, Reagan-Regan, Kemp-Kasten, and Bradley-Gephardt all fail to produce the much needed reforms they promise. Each simplifies the current system in only a minor way. Each is advertised as making the system fairer, but to a greater or lesser degree, each significantly fails to do this. Each taxes only income, leaving the great mass of individual and corporate wealth untaxed. It is an insidious deception to term a tax plan 'fair' or 'fairer' when it purposely avoids taxing wealth. In truth, each is merely cosmetic reform, different means for maintaining the status quo, or even widening the gap between rich and poor, when what is really needed is major surgery.

In terms of its economic role, it is useful to view the federal government as a giant electric utility. Without electricity our nation quickly grinds to a halt. The electric utility inputs coal or oil, processes it, and outputs electrical current to serve the general interest of society. In a like manner, the federal government inputs taxes, processes them in accordance with societal needs and laws, and outputs transfer payments. When input (taxes) to the federal utility are insufficient or inappropriate it distorts both the processing and the output, which is sufficient to retard economic and social development and to produce disastrous economic cycles. The Great Depression was in part the result of the underdeveloped role of the federal government in the economic affairs of our nation. The numerous recessions that have followed have also resulted from federal economic insufficiencies.

America can do much better than its current system of federal taxation, and better than the three proposals for reform that are currently being considered. If we continue to fuel the federal utility with less than the necessary amount of fuel and in inappropriate mixtures, we will continue to generate insufficient energy to power our advanced industrial economy.

Objectives

Metacapitalism's proposed Prosperity Revenue Act seeks to transform the very way we think about taxation from something that is evil and onerous, to something that is beneficial and a privilege. The Prosperity Revenue

Act returns sanity to taxation, and idle capital to an active economy. For those who experience temporary or permanent financial impairment, a firm "safety net" is established. By law all Americans will be entitled to a minimum level of financial security and guaranteed retirement with dignity. By law all Americans will be entitled to quality health care and higher education without immediate financial obligation. These important entitlements and more will be accomplished by means of **Metacapitalism's** proposed Income Security Act (ISA), National Medical Care Act (MCA), and National Education Act (NEA).

In sum, PRA will eliminate all tax deductions for individuals and businesses; institute a flat ten percent tax on the revenues of business and income of individuals; and expand the tax base by instituting a tax on individual and corporate wealth. Current and historical tax theory and practice emphasize the taxing of income over and above everything else, almost completely ignoring accumulated wealth. This is probably less an oversight than the deliberate mischief of those who create and enact our laws, most of whom are wealthy. Annual income in America, depending upon the way it is measured, is approximately $2.8 to $3.5 trillion. Accumulated wealth, though never appropriately inventoried, is estimated at $20 trillion to $25 trillion.

Metacapitalism's Prosperity Revenue Act is a substantial departure from both our current federal tax laws and the various alternative tax proposals that are now in circulation. **Metacapitalism's** system for taxation contains no compromises whatsoever, political or otherwise. It proposes a flat tax, one rate system, not only for individuals but also for incorporated and unincorporated businesses. It is a targeted tax that seeks to collect twenty-five percent of GNP by a combination of individual income tax, business revenue tax, excise taxes, inheritance tax, property tax, and wealth tax. Of the twenty-five percent of GNP collected (this does not include the property tax, most of which would be sent directly back to the various states and localities), seventy-five percent would be returned to the nation's citizenry in the form of monetary transfers, the bulk of which would take the form of a National Productivity Dividend. Of the twenty-five percent that would be retained for use by the federal government, approximately fifteen percent would be allocated to our national defense, and ten percent would be allocated to financing the operations of government.

As a targeted system for taxation, the Prosperity Revenue Act will allow taxpayers, individuals and businesses, to know in what proportion and just where federal transfers and spending are going. If the American electorate deems the percentage allocation to national defense too high or the allocation to the Productivity Dividend too low, they may and should vote to change it. Currently, citizens have only the remotest understanding of the true workings of the federal budgeting process, a process so complex and tainted by special interest considerations that it defies description, confounding even those in government who are most closely linked to it. By themselves setting federal budget allocations, the electorate may exercise its collective wisdom, and move from apathetic disinterest to active participation, taking another step toward a fuller implementation of a directed democracy and greater individual freedom.

Let us now turn to the specifics of **Metacapitalism's** proposed Prosperity Revenue Act, first by comparing the major categories of the current federal taxation system with **Metacapitalism's** proposed Prosperity Revenue Act, and then looking at who will come out ahead and who will be left behind.

A. *Exemptions.* Current law provides for $1,000 exemptions for self, spouse, each dependent, and for the blind and the elderly. Thus a family of four filing a joint return may exempt $4,000 from their federal taxes. A blind or elderly person living alone may exempt $2,000. The Prosperity Revenue Act provides for an exemption of 150 percent of the national poverty line. Thus, if poverty is established at $8,000 for an individual, then $12,000 would be exempted. There is no provision for joint tax returns. Thus, in a family each working member would file a tax return.

B. *Deductions for Individuals.* Current law provides an unwieldly array of ever-changing deductions such as the standard deduction, mortgage interest, personal interest, state and local taxes, charitable contributions, medical, two-earner, and so on. These deductions have led our nation's citizenry to a massive preoccupation with tax deductions, to language which differentiates between tax avoidance, deemed legal, and tax evasion, deemed illegal. The development of a picayune concern about taxes has impinged on our personal freedoms. The Prosperity Revenue Act eliminates all deductions for individuals.

C. *Deductions for Business.* There is currently gross confusion regarding business taxation. Businesses are taxed only if they earn a profit. Businesses that lose money pay no tax and are even given a deduction to offset future taxes. This is certainly a peculiar anomaly within the context of a free market, competitive, capitalistic system. Losers are subsidized by winners. The current tax system rewards the inefficient business and penalizes the efficient ones. This is a vivid example of the confusion that has beset our uncertain capitalism. Under current tax law, businesses are liable for taxes only on their profits, and thus they are encouraged to do everything possible to limit their tax liability. Since tax considerations weigh heavily on most major business decisions, decisions are often made that are defective in terms of the optimizations of production and distribution because tax considerations are considered primary.

Of late, businesses, particularly the giant corporations, have been paying less and less of their fair share of federal tax. As we have seen, tax deductions and loopholes are so plentiful that many giant corporations pay no tax at all. Prosperity Revenue Act will put an end to the vulgar irregularities that now plague the current business tax law. All deductions will be eliminated and instead of taxing businesses on their highly elusive profits, all businesses will be taxed on their gross revenues. After a period of adjustment, this will place each business on a competitive basis and, along with proposed massive corporate and financial reforms, serve to restore real competition and the benefits that accrue forthwith to the marketplace. To be a true market economy, then, we must remove interferences, obstructions, irregularities, and obstacles from the marketplace. The current business tax law allows all of these and more. If individuals can function well without a myriad of deductions, then so can corporations. By removing special interest deductions from the tax law, America's citizenry will take a giant step toward the realization of a government that serves the general and not the special interest.

D. *Income Indexing and Income Averaging.* Indexing income to reflect inflation and eliminate the effects of bracket creep was recently incorporated into the tax law. Income averaging allows those whose incomes vary greatly from year to year to adjust reported income to an average figure so that they are not taxed at the higher rate in any given year. Both of these features are beneficial under the current tax law but entirely unnecessary under the Prosperity Tax. Since there is a single tax rate that will vary only modestly from year to year, both features are superfluous.

E. *The Property Tax.* Under current law, property is not taxed uniformly by the federal government but by a confusion of irregular state and local laws. Each state and its several localities assesses the value of various personal and business, residential and recreational, urban and rural, public and private properties in their domains. Taxation is irregular and inconsistent, and often based on tradition. This usually means that old money does not pay its fair share of the property tax. A family's primary residence with a resale value of $100,000 may be taxed at a one percent rate in one locale, at two percent in another and at five percent in still another.

Property tax has been the traditional base for funding public education, and its gross distortions are instrumental in establishing the unequal quality of education in our country. As might be expected under current tax law, the children of upper income families receive a superior public school education, while the children of low income families receive a poor education characterized by disinterested teachers and underfunded curricula.

The Prosperity Revenue Act will transfer property taxation from the states to the federal government and uniform procedures for valuation, assessment, and collection would be implemented. Currently, approximately $125 billion a year is spent on public school education. A national figure per grade should be established, and, funds would be allocated according to an areas child population. The education of our children is too important to leave to the machinations of petty bureaucrats. The amount of money spent for the education of each child should be uniform across the land and continuously evaluated and adjusted to meet the demands of our increasingly complex world.

Currently, the amount spent each year for a child's public school education is approximately $4,000, with a high of $8,000 and a low of $2,000. The Prosperity Revenue Act would fix a percentage of Gross National Product to funding public school education. Currently, about 2.5 percent of GNP is earmarked for public school education.

The Prosperity Revenue Act would increase this to three percent and have that figure adjustable only by the direct vote of the citizenry.

F. *A Tax on Wealth.* Currently, except for a few states like Connecticut, there is no tax on individual or corporate wealth. In fact, the aggregate wealth of the nation, both public and private, is not precisely known. The Prosperity Revenue Act contains only one new tax and that is a five percent tax on wealth held by individuals (assets minus liabilities) in excess of $100,000. This includes bank accounts, stocks, bonds, land, personal property at current valuations, and all other investments. Wealth held by corporations would be subject to exactly the same tax. With this tax vast amounts of now idle capital will be put to work. By transforming idle wealth into active capital, the Prosperity Revenue Act will permanently adjust the economy upward, thus increasing the standard of living for all Americans.

G. *Retirement.* Very few of the current retirement vehicles offer retirement with dignity, and these to only a very small percentage of the nation's population. There is Social Security, the IRA and Keogh plans, and an assortment of private, corporate, and government pension plans. Social Security is by far the major retirement plan. It is essentially enforced payroll taxation, which has grown from $90.8 billion in 1976 to a projected $289.4 billion in 1986. Yet Social Security provides only the most modest retirement for our elderly, one unworthy of the contributions they have made to our nation. The Prosperity Revenue Act replaces Social Security with the Productivity Dividend, and taxes income accruing to other retirement plans on a current rather than a deferred basis. The Productivity Dividend increases by age, and thus, the most elderly are the most protected and rewarded. Currently, under Social Security a person retiring at age 65 would receive $660 a month. With the Productivity Dividend that same person would receive $1500 a month. Further, under Social Security, an 85 year old would receive the same $660 a month, whereas under the Prosperity Revenue Act and the Productivity Dividend that person would receive $2500 a month. America must not continue to ignore its elderly. We must recognize their contributions and see to it that the assurance that their dignified retirement is among our highest priorities.

H. *Investments.* A truly confusing array of tax deductions for various forms of investments characterizes our current special interest tax law. There is a capital gains exclusion, a lower tax rate for capital gains, a dividend exclusion, a homeowner exclusion, and an array of total exemptions for income derived from investments in general obligation and other municipal bonds. Because of the rather large loopholes in this area, several Americans with annual incomes exceeding $1 million a year have paid not one cent in federal taxes. The Prosperity Revenue Act totally eliminates all these deductions, taxing all income from such sources at the same single rate.

I. *Depreciation.* The current tax law includes an investment credit of six percent to ten percent and various methods for depreciating assets, some faster than others.

The Prosperity Revenue Act completely eliminates these deductions.

J. *Employer Provided Fringe Benefits.* Under current tax law, this area is marked by vast distortions and confusions. Several of the major fringe benefits are entirely excluded from federal taxation, such as health insurance and life insurance. Certain educational benefits are excluded, while others are taxed and the same is true of an assortment of other benefits, none more so than the corporate expense account. Since the Prosperity Revenue Act taxes revenue and not profit, corporations are free to provide employees with whatever fringe benefits they wish. Only direct income received by the employee is taxable under the Prosperity Revenue Act.

K. *Lower Income Provisions.* Current tax law excludes income derived from workers compensation insurance, taxes unemployment compensation if the recipient reports an annual income over $12,000, and provides an earned income credit and a child care credit. For consistency, and to move from complexity to simplicity, from a special interest orientation to concern for the general interest of the citizenry, under the Prosperity Revenue Act all income is taxed at a single rate. With the Productivity Dividend, all but the most intransigent poverty will be eliminated in America. And that poverty is best addressed with very specific programs and not the federal tax law.

L. *Tax Rates.* The current tax law contains fifteen progressively increasing rates for individuals peaking at fifty percent and a series of rates for corporations peaking at

159

forty-six percent. Because of the vast assortment of avoidances, loopholes, deductions, and the like, few, if any, now pay these maximum rates. They are more an illusion of fairness than a reality. Under the Prosperity Revenue Act individuals will pay a single rate of ten percent as established by the nation's National Economic Plan and as adjusted by the direct vote of the citizenry. Corporations and unincorporated businesses will pay a single rate of ten percent of gross revenue, subject to the same regulatory authority as the individual tax rate.

M. *Excise and Inheritance Taxes.* The Prosperity Revenue Act proposes a doubling of the federal excise tax. As regards inheritance, there would be a 100 percent tax on all inheritance exceeding $1 million and the tax on amounts less than $1 million would be a flat ten percent, with first $100,000 excluded.

N. *Penalties.* Since there are no tax deductions under the Prosperity Revenue Act, there can be no tax avoidances. Thus, failure to pay, unless mitigated in some way, is regarded as tax evasion and is a crime. Penalties for minor evasions should be moderate; an evasion of $1,000 to $5,000 will carry a penalty of 200 percent of the amount evaded for the first offense, a similar fine plus confiscation of fifty percent of property for a second offense, and full confiscation of property plus a one year jail term for the third offense. A moderate evasion, an amount between $5,001 and $25,000 will entail a 200 percent penalty plus a six month prison term for the first offense; seventy-five percent confiscation of property plus a one year prison term for the second offense and full confiscation of property plus a three year prison term for the third offense. Major evasions, amounts exceeding $25,000, will carry harsh sentences. Full confiscation of property plus a one year prison term for the first offense; full confiscation plus five years for the second, and full confiscation plus ten years for the third. Licensed professionals, twice convicted of minor or moderate evasions, will lose their license to practice upon their first conviction for a major evasion.

O. *Income Security* Current tax law was not designed with income security in mind. Except for a dozen or so programs targeted specifically to the poor, and unemployment insurance, which is a payroll tax to employers, the vast majority of Americans live completely unprotected with regard to income guarantees until they retire. Upon retirement, Social Security which is another payroll tax paid by employees, employers, and self-employed individuals, provides an extremely modest income. Medicare, which is a subsidized health insurance program for the elderly, covering twenty-eight million aged persons, has recently been rolled into Social Security. All these programs are significantly underfunded, improperly administered, and subject to the axe of neurotic conservatives.

Metacapitalism's proposed Prosperity Revenue Act is specifically designed to provide income security to all Americans. When coupled to **Metacapitalism's** proposed National Medical Care Act, the National Productivity Dividend eliminates the need for Social Security, Medicare, and unemployment insurance. And the remainder of so-called "Low-Income Benefit Programs" will be made

161

obsolete by these in tandem with *Metacapitalism's* proposed Community Participation Act, and National Education Act.

Obstacles

Just as the Voting Powers Act is necessary for the full-flowering of American democracy, the Prosperity Revenue Act is crucial for the revitalization of American capitalism. Those conservatives that will oppose VPA will also oppose PRA. That the humanitarian ideals and progressive instincts have been temporarily paralyzed by the insidious palaver of this tiny group is merely a function of many uncertainties that afflict both democracy and capitalism, and the paucity of proposals for empowering their further evolution.

There are no concrete obstacles to the enactment of the Prosperity Revenue Act. The passage of the Voting Powers Act all but guarantees passage of the Prosperity Revenue Act.

There are those who will responsibly argue that the transition from our current system of federal taxation to Prosperity Revenue will prove chaotic. To a degree they are right. But proper planning and a phased approach will certainly serve to mitigate most, if not all, of the imbalances that would ensue. Others will argue that the inventorying and valuation of property will prove difficult and unwieldy. There is some truth to this. But the severe confiscatory elements of PRA should serve nicely to protect society from those who would attempt to shield their wealth from valuation or perpetrate other tax frauds.

THE INCOME SECURITY ACT (ISA)

Introduction

In America's advanced industrial society there can be no real freedom for an individual or for the citizenry as a whole without income for everybody. Without an income, poverty, lurking in the wings, moves center stage and dominates the scene. Today, more than twenty-five percent of Americans live in or near poverty and a large percentage of these people are descendant of Africans. In America the importation of slaves was outlawed by an Act of Congress in April 1776. The new law rang hollow for the hundred thousand Africans already enslaved for nearly a century, until a combination of conscience and the Civil War provoked President Abraham Lincoln to deliver the Emancipation Proclamation on January 1, 1863, effectively freeing slaves in all the territories still at war with the Union.

Thus, nearly a full century elapsed before an espoused principle of freedom became a reality. But even now that principle is not fully realized. The two hundred years from the date of our historic Revolution have merely transformed the iron chains of our agrarian past to the bondage of poverty. Today, in the land of freedom, those who have never toiled are far richer than those who have toiled their entire lives. Less than five percent of the population controls more than ninety-five percent of the nation's wealth.

Metacapitalism's proposed Income Security Act aims to break, once and for all, the chains of actual and potential poverty that enslave the vast majority of Americans. ISA provides for a minimum guaranteed income and retirement with dignity for all citizens. It establishes the monthly payment of a National Productivity Dividend to all adult Americans (over the age of twenty-five) which will significantly reduce the rate and threat of poverty as well as consigning to history the dehumanizing experiences of welfare and unemployment payments, and the deficiencies of the Social Security System.

Background

In 1935 Congress passed the Social Security Act (SSA), which provided retirement income to persons upon reaching the age of sixty-five, and a single-sum death benefit to surviving families. Approximately sixty percent of the American labor force was covered until the early 1950s when SSA was expanded to include the whole workforce except for certain ,federal, state, and local government employees who were already covered by superior retirement plans. In 1956 Congress again expanded

SSA to include benefits for disabled workers and lowered the retirement age for women to sixty-two (optional and with reduced benefits). The early retirement option was also given to men. Payments by SSA to retirees are called benefits even though a mandatory payroll tax is used to fund the plan. In 1981 the average retiree received approximately $400 a month from Social Security as contrasted with average monthly non-farm income of $1100, hardly what could be termed retirement with dignity.

With the exception of our national defense, Social Security is by far the largest of all government programs, and in 1981 represented nearly seven percent of all disposable personal income. The estimated value of the current aggregate Social Security entitlement and estimated future entitlements for workers currently covered exceeds $30 trillion in 1984 dollars.

In 1946, eleven years after passing SSA, Congress passed the Full Employment Act (FEA). FEA committed government to the pursuit of economic policies that would contain future unemployment levels to no more than three to four percent of the workforce, a level deemed acceptable by a consensus of economists and politicians. Yet, since passage of FEA, except for brief respites in the early 1950s and the late 1960s, the unemployment rate in America has been consistently higher than the three to four percent acceptability level established by FEA. In fact, the long-term trend in American unemployment is definitely an upward one. It was 4.9 percent in 1975, 8.5 percent in 1977, 7.1 percent in 1978, 6.1 percent in 1979, 5.8 percent in 1980, 7.1 percent in 1981, 7.6 percent in 1982, and actually climbed above 10 percent in 1983, averaging 9.7 percent for the entire year.

In America, in 1982, there were 10.5 million officially unemployed persons. In addition, there were 62 million potentially employable people who were not counted as part of the official labor force. Of these, 55.5 million did not then want jobs, while 6.5 million did. Of the 55.5 million who did not want jobs, 6.4 million were in school, 4 million were ill or disabled, 28.4 million were keeping house, and 12.3 million were retired. Of the 6.5 million who did want jobs, 1.7 million were in school, 0.7 million were ill or disabled, 1.4 million were keeping house, 1.6 million thought that for a variety of reasons they could not get a job, and 1.1 million listed other reasons.

If the 6.5 million people who wanted a job in 1982 but were not actively seeking one are added to the 10.7 million who were officially unemployed, there were a total of 17.3 million Americans unemployed as against approximately 100 million employed. Regardless of the way you choose to measure unemployment, it must be conceded that the objectives of the Full Employment Act of 1946 have been ignored or abandoned.

In June of 1983 the government reported that nearly twelve million Americans were officially unemployed, 6.3 million of whom were males and 4.8 million were females; white unemployment was 8.4 million; black unemployment was 2.4 million; Hispanic unemployment was .87 million. The respective rates of unemployment for white, black and Hispanic were 8.6%, 20.6%, and 14.0%. Long-term unemployment rates soared for whites and have skyrocketed for the black and Hispanic minorities. Real unemployment is estimated to be fifty percent higher than that officially reported by the government, and if those who work for wages at or near the poverty line were added to the unemployment rate, it would rise to nearly half of America's employable population.

Currently a one percent rise in the rate of unemployment means that approximately one million additional Americans are without work. An official ten percent unemployment rate means than ten million Americans are officially unemployed and that possibly as many as twenty million are unemployed, meaning that nearly twenty-five percent of our total population is without a sustained income.

Something is very wrong with employment in America when our official unemployment rate is now averaging approximately eight percent for the five-year period from 1979 to 1983, and the unofficial rate is likely double that, and moreover the ninety percent of employed Americans are somewhere between intolerably and moderately dissatisfied with the nature of their work.

Beyond Social Security, which is essentially a mediocre retirement fund, and the Full Employment Act of 1946, which is gathering considerable dust in the basement of Congress, and a miscellany of temporary unemployment benefits, private pension plans, and local welfare programs, there is nothing in America either now existent or on the drawing boards to counter the long-term trend in the rise of unemployment, to protect our citizenry from severe economic hardship, or to provide a dignified retirement for workers. Social Security is the largest asset of most American families, the primary source of retirement funds. But an income of one-third of their average annual wage is not only not satisfactory, but borders on the inhumane.

In searching for the cause of the rising trend of unemployment in America and other advanced industrial economies we need not employ sophisticated economic sleuths armed with intricately mathematicized econometric models and high-speed computers. The handwriting was already on the wall when automation began to replace human labor, when computers invaded business, and when modern farming techniques began to vastly increase yields per acre. As modern economies grow in sophistication, as automated assembly lines, integrated circuits, robots, and fertilizers are substituted for human toil, there will be fewer and fewer traditional employment opportunities. And when the situation is further exacerbated by a steadily rising population (from 1970 to 1982 the civilian labor force in America grew from 82.8 million to 110.2 million), you have everything needed for a permanent rise in the rate of unemployment.

In America, there has also been a tendency to export labor intensive jobs to countries such as Korea, Haiti, and Taiwan whose labor supply demands a far lower wage. Were it not for the rapid rise of many trivial occupations in the personal service sector of America's economy, the rate of unemployment would now, more than likely, exceed the topmost level of the Great Depression. Massive unemployment and the twin corollaries—severe social dislocation and economic deprivation—are a very real threat to America's citizenry. Another Great Depression, or worse, looms as a far more likely eventuality than the possibility of a direct Soviet military incursion or invasion. The possibility of a direct Soviet military challenge is remote because of our awesome military and retaliatory power. The Soviet leadership will not risk incineration in pursuit of its geo-political, ideological, and economic ambitions. And they need not. American capitalism has reached a state of such advanced development that the continued growth of the giant corporations, the economic monopolists, and the mammoth industrial and financial conglomerates, if left unchecked, will soon finish the job of destroying competition and freedom in America.

Almost everything has been perceived as American capitalism's antagonist except for the real antagonist. The greatest defilers of freedom and competition in America are our giant corporations, run usually by surrogates to further the interests of dynasties in America. With unusual vigor, America's professional executives argue the merits of our free enterprise system to enhance their public image, while privately they fund political action committees (PACs) to promote their special interests, lobby for special tax concessions, tariffs, quotas, regulations, and government loans and daily violate the spirit of our nation's antitrust laws. In America today, no person is entirely protected for the consequences of an economic disaster. It is possible that those who have toiled toward a secure retirement will find themselves ruined by depression and a bankrupted Social Security fund. American capitalism requires mass markets, a multitude of citizens with income to spend, an army of consumers. It is consumption that ignites capitalism and consumption requires money. How long will it take us to realize that denying income to certain segments of our society benefits no one and hurts us all. Those who are now denied an income, the unemployed, those who live in or near poverty, the under-employed, and the middle classes who live comfortable lives, all are suffering an unnecessary exposure to prospective deprivation because our economists and legislators will not modernize economic theories, the institutional infrastructure, and the socioeconomic programs and policies that have made American capitalism uncertain.

Ironically, before the evolution of capitalism, the many produced primarily for the few—the serfs farmed the land of the aristocracy. The lion's share of the crops and cattle was devoured by the feudal lord and his vassals; only a small percentage of what was produced went to the peasant-serfs, barely enough to sustain life. With the evolution of capitalism, however, the production-distribution differential was considerably changed. With capitalism, the many produced primarily for their own consumption, and the capitalist extracted only a small percentage of the total. But, given the enormous increases in productive capacity, the huge numbers of people employed in production, this small percentage was quite a powerful sum. The new capitalist grew far wealthier than his predecessor, the feudal lord.

As matters stand now, only employment provides an income for the vast majority of Americans. Thus, income which derives directly from employment is the spark that ignites capitalism's engine. But what will happen to our people, our nation, to democracy in general if that spark fizzles or dies? What will happen if long-term hyper-unemployment (twenty percent or more) strikes? Given the current trends in our economy, the uncertainty of capitalism, the unchecked destruction of competition by the economic monopolists, the drift away from labor intensive employment, the exportation of jobs and capital, and the massive growth of trivial employment, such hyper-unemployment may strike at any time, for any number of reasons or causes.

Only once, during the Great Depression, has America experienced hyper-unemployment. And even then, when our economy was far smaller, our population far less, our international interdependence almost nonexistent, the horror was deep and pervasive. Those who had been rich were instantly impoverished. Suicide was common. Hunger was prevalent. In every city there were "soup kitchens" to help feed long lines of hungry, homeless people. The official unemployment rate was pegged at twenty-five percent, but was probably far higher.

The Great Depression lasted for over a decade and did not abate until government became active in the economy. Almost every American suffered, but most survived. Today, the likelihood is that many would perish. The greater complexities that now underlie our economy will

171

inhibit corrective actions. A quick fix is impossible. Given these potentialities and governing parameters, it is unthinkable that we should not move now to redirect the course of American capitalism. Now is the time to correct the mistaken economic theories, policies, and programs that have engulfed the American economy, transformed vibrance into stagnation, and submerged us in a swamp of mediocrity.

Objectives

It should come as no surprise that the single most important factor in maintaining a prosperous advanced industrial economy is the economic role played by government. At the time of the Great Depression our economy was entirely free of governmental influences, there was no macroeconomic theory, and governmental revenue was a miniscule $2.8 billion to $4 billion a year for the entire period from 1921 to 1930. For each year of the decade leading up to the Great Depression the federal government actually ran a surplus. Thus, it was a combination of a lack of governmental influence in the national economy, an insufficient body of economic theory, governmental surpluses, and hyper-speculation that brought about the Great Depression. It was not until government became active in the affairs of the economy that the back of the Great Depression was finally broken.

American capitalism is stagnating not because business lacks ideas, energy, or incentives, but because the role of the federal government in national economic affairs is more and more confused and uncertain. Our fear of being compared to the Soviets is so great that our national economic strategy has been prevented from evolving. ISA will be instrumental in helping to allay these fears because its centerpiece, the payment of a Productivity Dividend to all adult Americans, is a totally revolutionary concept and thus may not be confused with anything smacking of communism or socialism.

The Productivity Dividend is, essentially, a two-way monetary transfer—first from the nation's taxpayers by way of the Prosperity Revenue Act to government, and then from government to the American citizenry. It is a fundamental entitlement to all Americans. Eligibility and payment begin at age twenty-five and continue through retirement to death. Every citizen, rich and poor alike, will receive the monthly Productivity Dividend payment by direct electronic transfer. The dividend will initially be set to use approximately seventy-five percent of governmental revenue and increase over time to eighty percent as the economy prospers. The remaining twenty to twenty-five percent of governmental revenue will be used to fund governmental operations and remaining social programs.

Let us examine just how the Productivity Dividend would be raised and disbursed in the year 1986. We shall assume (1) enactment of *Metacapitalism's* Prosperity Revenue Act; (2) a GNP of $4.3 trillion, and (3) forty-nine percent of GNP will flow through to the federal government in the following way: $650 billion from a flat ten percent tax on corporate revenues and individual income; $1.25 trillion from a five percent tax on accumulated wealth; $108.6 billion from excise and inheritance taxes, and miscellaneous fees; and $125 billion from the transfer of state and local property taxation to the federal government.

Thus, hypothetically in the year 1986, the revenue flow to the federal government will total roughly $2.1 trillion. From the $2.1 trillion, $1.075 trillion, approximately fifty percent, will be directly transferred back to America's citizens as income and retirement supplements. This is the National Productivity Dividend in action.

We shall assume further an eligible population of 100 million, which shall be segmented into three groups: 45 million 25-44 year olds; 35 million 45-64 year olds; and 20 million aged 65 and over.

Senior citizens would receive approximately three times the amount on an individual basis as those just becoming eligible for the Productivity Dividend. There are three reasons for this. First, the Productivity Dividend replaces Social Security as a retirement fund and is created to provide retirement with dignity for all Americans. Second, the older one becomes, the more one is entitled to reap the common benefits of American citizenship. Third, younger citizens are generally less needy than the elderly. If the allocation is divided according to a two-ninths, three-ninths, four-ninths split, this results in monthly payments of $377, $765, and $1,790 respectively for each group. Alternately, by splitting the dividend in thirds, the respective allocations are $662, $851, and $1490.

Using the latter split, a married couple over age sixty-five would receive $2980 a month, far more than what they could expect from Social Security. Another married couple in the 45-64 age grouping would receive $1702 a month, a substantial income supplement that would be a hedge against unemployment, or, perhaps, means with which to shift life styles with the approach of middle age. In group one the monthly income supplement of $1324 for couples will serve to supplement income and provide security against the ravages of sudden unemployment.

The mere promise of the Productivity Dividend will energize America's economy for decades to come. All but the most intransigent poverty will be entirely eliminated, as will the bureaucracies and uncertainties that currently attend such existing programs as Social Security, welfare, and unemployment insurance. Freedom in America will be immeasurably increased as the entire citizenry is freed from income insecurities. Yet, incentives to produce will remain in place because, for most citizens, the Productivity Dividend will be only supplemental and not a complete income.

Every citizen will share in and reap the benefits of an expanding and increasingly prosperous economy. Wage slavery will come to an end as many Americans abandon trivial employments in favor of more rewarding occupations. Those who choose to remain in unrewarding occupations will find that their wage will rise significantly as more and more employers bid for less and less available labor.

As every adult citizen will automatically receive the Productivity Dividend, the rich may no longer argue that they support the poor, which will serve to reduce the current polarization between the two groups. The only qualifications upon the receipt and expenditure of the Productivity Dividend would be that up until age sixty-five the entire sum must be spent each month; that those who are imprisoned will have their dividend revoked for the term of their imprisonment; and that those citizens who make use of *Metacapitalism's* proposed National Medical Care Act will use not more than $1000 a year from the dividend to defray medical expenses (this is merely to deter the hypochondriacs). Other than these qualifications, the sole remaining condition is that each citizen not only register, but also vote in each national election.

Conclusion

The Productivity Dividend will place a permanent tarpaulin under the American citizenry that will protect all from the horrors of economic dislocations, deal a devastating blow to the Hobbesian construction of "survival of the fittest" (a degeneratively brutish construction at best), free many of our citizenry from menial work, loosen the bonds that tie the impoverished to city ghettoes, and enable all Americans to glory in the new spirit that will permeate America, the spirit of a new humanism.

THE POLITICAL REFORM ACT

Introduction

The Political Reform Act seeks to modernize and streamline the federal government so that it will function more efficiently, better serve the general interests of the American citizenry, and become more responsible and responsive to the mandates of the American electorate.

Background

The Voting Powers Act enables the American electorate to initiate and enact federal legislation. The Prosperity Revenue Act transforms the federal taxation system from an indefensible monstrosity into a simple, fair, and efficient system while greatly expanding the tax base. The Income Security Act provides adult Americans with a minimum guaranteed income in the form of a Productivity Dividend, thus freeing workers from wage slavery and providing a dignified retirement to all. It also eliminates or greatly reduces much of the special interest-oriented federal bureaucracy.

177

But, there still remains the anachronistic bicameral federal legislature, the overly politicized and increasingly moribund Supreme Court, and electoral processes that allow too many elections and are thus extremely wasteful, imbalanced in favor of special interests, and cosmetic in their approach and appeal. The federal government has become a colossal, self-directed behemoth. What America needs is a sleek, citizen-directed, humanitarian government. America can no longer afford to suffer the blockages to our institutional infrastructure that result directly from our archaic bicameralism and from the misbegotten and naively legalistic meanderings of our highest court. Rather than being the checks and balances they were intended to be, the House of Representatives and the Supreme Court are the willful and unwitting promoters of narrow special interest groups. For a variety of reasons, institutional reorganization, though fraught with difficulties, is urgent. American industry has always faced up to the arduous but beneficial task of massive reorganization. The federal government, though it is reluctant to reform, has reached the point of no return. It must soon reorganize or perish from its own overweight.

Objectives

The most urgent objective of the Political Reform Act is the elimination of that vast institutional blockage, the House of Representatives. For too long this legislative body has failed to perform any positive function for the

American people and has, instead, catered to the needs of a myriad of special interest groups whose common denominator is wealth and whose common goal is maintenance of the status quo. Much that carried the foul smell of political favoritism or political corruption emanates from the House of Representatives.

The motive which gave rise to the creation of a bicameral legislature, i.e. to provide a balance between the representation afforded property owners in the Senate and that given to more populous states in the House, is now seriously out of date. If it ever served its intended purpose, it is now more an illusion of justice than reality.

The concepts of one person, one vote and proportional representation (more populous states having a proportionately greater vote at the federal level than less populous states) are still sound. And, fortunately, they can be had without the burden of 435 members of the House of Representatives.

These 435 House members must run for re-election every two years. Just the time they spend campaigning, raising campaign funds, and hiring and training their staffs would be enough to render them ineffective. And, although the salary for this job is $72,600 a year, the average House member spends upwards of $100,000 on his or her campaign, with some spending more than $1,000,000. With campaign expenditures reaching these extraordinarily high levels, it is likely that the influence of Political Action Committees (PACs), privately funded lobbying organizations representing well-financed special interests, will continue to grow beyond its already high level. The very thought that the votes of our so-called elected repre-sentatives may be bought for cash or other pledges is repugnant. That the practice of buying these votes is widespread is a flagrant violation of democratic ideals, and it must be stopped immediately.

There is already a discernible movement among established democracies away from bicameral and towards unicameral legislatures. America should add to the momentum by abolishing the House of Representatives and replacing it with an additional Senator from each state in the Senate. This Senator, instead of campaigning for office, would be appointed by the state's governor and serve at his or her will. The proportional aspect of the House would be taken into account by proportioning the voting power of each of the 150 Senators to match the population of their home state in accordance with the lat-est national census.

The elimination of the House of Representatives and the addition of fifty additional senatorial appointees yields a net reduction of one entire legislative body, 385 legislators, and 435 congressional elections. 150 Senators are still too many legislators, but 150 is an improvement on 535.

A second objective of the Political Reform Act is the restructuring of the Supreme Court. Here blockage to our institutional infrastructure results from a reason opposite to that of the legislative branch; too few, instead of too many Justices. Instead of nine Justices, as at present, there should be fifteen. And instead of life terms, they should each be appointed to a single twelve-year term.

And instead of all being appointees of the President, only five should be presidential appointees; five should be appointed by the Senate, and the remaining five should be appointed by a vote of the fifty governors. The appointing of Senators by state governors (already a practice when there is a vacancy) and Supreme Court Justices (already a practice at state level) serves both to spread federal power back to the states and the general electorate, and to give the governors of the fifty states a far greater voice in national affairs.

Another much needed reform to the Supreme Court is in the area of appointing only judges and lawyers to serve. This practice is repugnant, highly discriminatory, and distorting. It is unacceptable that the law of the land be mainly created by lawyers in the legislature, and then interpreted by lawyers in the courts. That the law of the land has become almost the exclusive domain of lawyers has served in many instances to distort the law: legalisms are given greater weight than humanitarian considerations. The law of the land in America heavily favors property rights over human rights. The law in America is less concerned with justice than with legalisms. Justice as an American ideal is not extensively taught in America's law schools because if it were the grave disparity between the ideal and the reality would be all too evident.

By making sure that no more than seven of the Justices of the Supreme Court are lawyers, the overly legalistic bent of the law would be remedied; and new perspectives, emanating from something other than legal precedent, would be introduced.

The third and final objective of the Political Reform Act is to align the term of office of the Presidency with that of the Senate and to limit Senators to two six-year terms, instead of the unlimited number of terms they may now serve. A two-term Presidency seems perfectly appropriate, given the political complexities and demands of the day, and what is good for the executive branch should prove beneficial for the Senate and thus the country. A four-year presidential term is too short and should be extended to conform to the six-year term of the Senate. Thus, both the President and the 150 Senators would serve at most two six-year terms and Justices of the Supreme Court would serve a single twelve-year term.

Conclusion

Beyond an apathetic citizenry, the army of irate lawyers and judges, the 435 House members, their families and staffs, the PACs, and everyone related to, affiliated with, or somehow beholden to the stalwart guardians of the status quo, there are no concrete obstacles to enactment of the Political Reform Act. If a much younger America could free herself from the vice of foreign rule, rid itself of human bondage, and create an enormous middle class of income earners, then a much older America can certainly free itself from the dysfunction that emanates from the various institutional blockages at the federal level.

THE NATIONAL EDUCATION ACT (NEA)

Introduction

The continuing development of America's advanced industrial economy and the very evolution of American capitalism and democracy are heavily dependant on the educational preparedness of Americans. Two major flaws in the institutional infrastructure of our education system serve to deny equal educational opportunities to young Americans. There are many other problems, but the two dealt with here are disruptive of the entire educational process.

The first is the system of local property taxation which gives the children of well-to-do families educational advantages over the children of low and middle income families. The second is the patchwork system of funding higher education, which also favors the children of the rich. Not only does this frustrate the fulfillment of equal educational opportunity, it also places severe burdens on millions of American households as they struggle with the enormous costs of their children's higher education.

Background

The myth of equal opportunity in America is nowhere more apparent than in education. In the nineteenth century, America led the world in offering free quality education to all its children. Prior to this time, only the offspring of privileged classes could afford schooling. Yet, ironically, in the twentieth century, many factors have surfaced to undercut America's previously unparalleled record of educational opportunity, and promise to undermine the entire future of American education. Every American child is legally entitled to an education through high school. But because of massive inequities in the collection and distribution of property taxes (the primary source of secondary level educational funding) an American child's education is once again a function of the income of its parents.

The current system for financing secondary education gerrymanders poor children into public school districts receiving far less funding than those attended by children of the rich. Whereas upwards of $6,000 a year is spent on the high school education of pupils in well-to-do areas, less than $3,000 a year is spent on the children of poorer families. These inequities continue right up through America's colleges and universities. While the current patchwork system of financing does provide some financial relief (in the form of student loans, lower cost public universities, and an assortment of scholarships), by and large only America's wealthiest families can afford to send their children to college. In 1985 one year at Princeton University cost $15,000, $13,200 at the University of Rochester, $15,000 at Stanford, $14,500 at Wesleyan, and slightly more than half these figures at the University of California at Los Angeles, which is public. For middle income families these costs, which have tripled since 1975 while wages have remained stagnant, are truly burdensome. Many such families are forced to extreme sacrifice to help finance their children's university education. Others have simply given up, or help one child and not the other. For low income families these costs are impossible. Only the strongest and brightest children from low income families may reasonably expect to attend university, and then only with a wide range of assistance and part-time employment, both of which can be physically debilitating and personally degrading.

The financing of our educational system is unfair because it places the burden of paying for education on the family, when the true recipient of the benefits of education is society itself. Americans must once again realize that the right to an equal education for all is not only constitutionally guaranteed, but also the responsibility of a society to itself. An educated citizenry is the greatest protection freedom can have. Education begins in the home. Here those of fortunate birth receive their first social advantages. Those who suffer from disadvantages should not have to see them perpetuated in secondary and higher education. Equal access to education in America is a social responsibility, to the young, to freedom, to society itself.

Objectives

The main objective of NEA is to provide all Americans with equal access to a quality education, beginning with the secondary schools and continuing through undergraduate and graduate school. NEA does not seek to tamper with the competitive aspects of educational processes, though in all areas of testing a certain archaic rigidity which seems to favor the wealthy prevails. The equal access provision of NEA, as here written, is exclusively concerned with the availability of funds for educational purposes.

The funding of equal access education for all of America's youth involves two parts. The first part is the transfer of secondary school funding from states and localities to the federal government. At the moment, funds for public secondary schools are derived primarily from state and local property taxes. The abuses of this patchwork system of taxation are many and widespread. NEA proposes that both the assessment and collection of property taxes be shifted from the states and localities to the federal government, where uniform procedures would be implemented. Property tax assessment and collection would be actuarially derived in accordance with uniform assessment standards. Collections would be assured, and all monies so raised would be immediately allocated back to the states based on student population.

The second part of assuring equal access to educational opportunities for all involves the implementation of a fully vouchered system for funding higher education.

Federal vouchers would replace personal payment of tuition, room, board, books, and miscellaneous expenses. Coverage would be so complete that no student would be forced away from his or her studies into menial employment for the sake of financing education. A student with one or more part-time jobs to help pay his or her way may benefit by way of character development, but usually loses in terms of intensity to study. And certain curricula, particularly those in the physical sciences, are so demanding that part-time employment has a decisively negative impact on the student's ability to study intensively.

As with each of **Metacapitalism's** legislative initiatives, and in keeping with its general interest orientation, federal vouchers for the funding of higher education would be available to all American students regardless of need. Repayment of vouchers would start as soon as a student began his or her career. Such repayment would be actuarially derived based on lifetime income, exclusive of the Productivity Dividend, and take the form of two percent for undergraduate degrees, four percent for graduate degrees, and six percent for post-graduate degrees. Repayment over the student's lifetime, without the burdensome interest rates that characterize current student loans, reduces greatly the burden of repayment at the time the student first enters the workforce, when earnings are typically at their lowest levels and families are being formed.

NEA also addresses two other aspects of our current educational infrastructure which inhibit equal opportunity and are highly wasteful of our most precious resource, the human being. The first of these is the thousands of college admissions procedures; the second is the maturity level of students entering college.

NEA proposes that students apply directly to a newly formed National University Entrance Center (NUEC) that would replace the admissions offices at the thousands of colleges and universities around the country. NUEC, essentially a computerized admissions system overseen by a rotating board of university deans, would process a student's university admissions application, matching it against every appropriate opening in the country on a competitive basis as well as the student applicant's choices. Students would then be given a broad array of choices, an opportunity not currently available. It would also serve to eliminate favoritism, prejudice, and corruption emanating from the existing process, while optimizing the allocation of human and educational resources.

Today, many American colleges and universities allocate a disproportionate number of freshmen openings to the children of America's perceived elite; those who have attended expensive private schools, and those whose parents are wealthy or otherwise seen as powerful. The universities uniformly deny such discriminatory practices in their admissions procedures, but on the Op-Ed page of *The New York Times* a former registrar at Brown University confesses as much. It is high time that the current caretakers of our nation's educational infrastructure eliminate these evils, and while they are at it put an end to the monopolistic practice of tenure, which accomplishes precisely the opposite of its purported intent.

Current university admissions practices are highly wasteful of human resources and are also discriminatory. Perhaps even more wasteful are the students themselves, many of whom have not sufficiently matured upon graduating from high school and leaving the protection of their families to take full advantage of the educational opportunities at their disposal. NEA proposes that before entering college each student-applicant work for one year at community service. Such community service will give the student a one-year break from his or her studies, an opportunity to perform public service, build character, confidence, and perspective; all important elements of a good general education.

THE NATIONAL MEDICAL CARE ACT (MCA)

Introduction

Medical care is a major industry in America. Nearly eleven percent of the GNP, about $400 billion, is spent on hospital care, on physicians, drugs, dentists, nursing homes, administration, public health, and a variety of miscellaneous items. However, only America, among the major industrialized nations, is without a guaranteed national health care plan. As the following table clearly portrays, the cost of medical care in America rose from $13.2 billion in 1950 to $400 billion in 1984.

The funding to finance this huge expenditure is primarily derived from three sources: the federal government, corporations as insurance purchasers for employees, and private citizens paying their own bills.

Federal financing is derived from tax receipts, personal and corporate income tax, and a separate payroll tax for Medicare. Medicare and Medicaid are both floundering in fiscal turmoil as the cost of medical care is rising far more rapidly than anticipated, while Social Security tax

Medical Industry Revenue for the Selected Years
1950, 1960, 1970, 1978, and 1984.
(In billions of dollars)

Revenue Type	Selected Years				
	1950	1960	1970	1978	1984
Hospital care	4	10	28	76	150
Physician services	3	6	15	35	80
Drugs	2	4	9	15	35
Dental services	1	2	5	13	30
Nursing homes	0.2	0.5	5	16	35
Miscellaneous*	3	5	15	37	70
Percentage of GNP	4.5%	5.3%	7.8%	9.1%	10.8%
Medical industry income in billions of dollars.............	13.2	27.5	77	192	400

*Miscellaneous includes $4 billion in 1984 for medical research, and expenditures for public health and medical administration.

increases have not nearly kept pace. The combined federal expenditure for Medicare and Medicaid (including $50 billion in tax subsidies) in 1984 was approximately $150 billion, about 37 percent of the $400 billion total expenditure. Corporations paid $100 billion for employee medical insurance and individuals either as purchasers of medical insurance or as direct purchasers of medical services paid the $150 billion balance.

Given the current state of its entrenched bureaucracy, its organizational disarray, the selfishness of many of its medical practitioners, and its demonstrated inability to audit or correct itself, only a fundamental restructuring will rescue the medical industry from its self-destructive

Medical Industry Revenue for 1984

Where it comes from . . .
(in billions of dollars)

Government programs:	Private sector funds:
Medicare $59	Direct patient programs.....$85
Federal medicaid payments .$19	Private health insurance ...$110
Other federal health programs.........$25	Philanthropy...............$11
State medicaid payments ...$16	
Other state and local government programs $30	

Where it goes . . .
(in billions of dollars)

Hopsital care..	$147
Physician services	$69
Research, construction, administration, etc.	$42
Nursing home care..	$29
Other health care goods and services	$68

tendencies and prepare a suitable foundation for a more effective and more equitable delivery of health care services.

Without a formalized plan for national health care, America has defaulted into a de facto health care delivery system that is chaotic, ineffective and hampered by bureaucracy.

Except for some grumbling by physicians over remuneration, the experience of other nations that have already converted to some type of formalized national health care plan has been positive. In Britain, the National Health

Service owns most of the country's hospitals and negotiates contracts with physicians for patient care; funding is almost entirely provided by the general tax revenue. In Canada, the federal government makes grants to the various provinces who in turn run their own programs, handle the specifics of administration, reimbursement, and supplementary benefits which vary from province to province. In West Germany, France, and the Netherlands, health care is financed primarily by health insurance funds which enroll beneficiaries and process medical claims. These "sickness funds" are financed primarily by a national payroll tax, and deficits, as they arise, are funded from the general tax revenue. The Norwegian, Swedish, and Danish systems are variations of the above. In fact, there are many features in common between the American, Canadian, and European national health systems.

Within these systems, overall expenditures varies from a high of 9.7 percent of the GNP in West Germany in 1975 to a low of 5.6 percent in the United Kingdom, with the United States coming in at about an average for the group at 8.4 percent. The most striking difference between these nations with a national plan for medical care and our *ad hoc* American system is that those excluded from coverage in other lands tend to be the rich who have the option to purchase medical insurance rather than the poor, who cannot afford even basic coverage.

Unfortunately, no other nation can provide us with an adequate model or plan for our national health care. If we are to achieve a fundamental restructuring of our medical industry and national health care system, we must innovate. We are accustomed to reorganizing major corporations, even entire industries, and we are adept at creating new financial instruments. Now we must apply our organizational skills and financial prowess to the rescue of our medical industry and to the creation of a guaranteed national health care plan.

Background

Over the past decade there have been several national health care proposals presented to Congress, most notably Health Care for All Americans, sponsored by Senator Edward Kennedy, and the National Health Plan, sponsored by the administration of President Jimmy Carter. Though each is well-intentioned and extends medical coverage to the entire population, each contains serious flaws. Neither plan deals adequately with those problems inherent in the medical industry that have led to significant inflation of medical costs. Neither plan cuts through the bureaucracy and monopolism that attends the medical industry, and each may, in fact, be seen as further exacerbating the inflation that, since 1960, has been double that of the Consumer Price Index. The flaws in our medical industry are serious; they are structural flaws that have led the medical profession into a vast betrayal of the American people.

The crises in American health care will not be solved by throwing money at it. Eleven percent of the GNP is already more than sufficient funding flowing to the medical industry, and, given the rampant monopolism, greed, gross incompetence, and organizational disarray everywhere prevalent, the physician is not inclined or able to heal himself. The license to practice medicine and dentistry has become more of a license to steal than a license to heal. And it has been noted that ten to twenty percent of the 450 thousand active physicians in private and public practice are functioning with major impairments, are incompetent, or are drug addicts. Self-regulation within the medical industry is a mockery. Rarely does a doctor inform supervisory boards of impairment, incompetence, or drug addiction he or she has observed, even though such manifestations are potentially life-threatening. Bogus physicians without any medical training practice unrestrained, unnoticed by qualified physicians.

The primary problem afflicting America's medical industry is excessive cost. As we have already seen, the aggregate bill for medical and related treatment now consumes eleven percent of the GNP and is rising at more than twice the rate of the Consumer Price Index. Medical expenditure, $400 billion annually, now exceeds national defense spending and the expenditure for secondary and higher education combined.

Although the medical industry is as decentralized as any in America, it is dominated by monopolism. For the most part the practice of medicine in America is an uncontrolled monopoly. American citizens are free to defend themselves in a court of law but not to write a simple prescription for previously diagnosed ailments.

Most visits to doctors' offices are unnecessary— involving complaints that could be dealt with over the telephone or by the patient himself. Doctors run no risks in prescribing for their patients an enormous array of unnecessary tests and medicines; surgical procedures and hospital care are abused in order to enrich physicians and hospital owners. The maxim "Let the buyer beware," is truly applicable to the medical profession. But the American public appears to be either too spoiled by medical insurance or too timid to voice its protests. In every instance, monopolistic practices lead to excessive costs, inefficient operation, and the suppression of opportunities for employment and innovation.

Many other factors, besides monopolism, have lead to the vast escalation of medical costs. Medical insurance has created a powerful incentive for many otherwise rational spenders to consume excessive amounts of medical treatment. They would be more prudent if forced to pay for these facilities from their own funds. Coincidentally, these same insurance funds have led doctors to authorize medical procedures that are either redundant, inefficient, or purely sham. The first question asked a prospective patient is not "What's wrong?" or "How are you feeling?" but rather "What sort of insurance do you have?"

The price of physician charges for his services is subject to wide variances. Patients are usually too timid and ill-informed to question a doctor about fees or negotiate a lower fee. Thus the patient is unable either to determine professional integrity or the lack of it or professional fairness in financial matters.

Beyond encouraging much excessive and unwarranted medical care various private medical insurers have fueled medical inflation by making their own significant profits from the medical industry in order to cover the vast clerical bureaucracies they need to process insurance enrollments and medical claims. These medical insurance bureaucracies, coupled with the hodgepodge of inconsistent federal, state, and local health care regulations, add to inefficiencies and high costs.

Though in itself a welcome development, the increased life expectancy of the American citizenry is also a factor in the soaring health care costs. Because of the new aversion to smoking and other pollutants and vices, increased attention to diet and exercise, and advanced in medical technology, Americans are living longer. The life expectancy for American women has increased from 68.7 years in 1950 to 77.9 years in 1984; for American men the figures constitute an increase from 66.2 in 1950 to 69.5 in 1984. A longer life means greater medical expense because a far greater amount is spent on medical care by senior citizens than by younger segments of the population.

The monopolism, the medical insurers, longer life expectancy, advances in medical care technology, and the federal government all share the responsibility for escalating medical care expenditures. With the enactment of Medicare and Medicaid, medical care for the poor and the elderly has been greatly increased and improved. Both

Medicare and Medicaid are important and necessary pieces of social legislation, but each was enacted as an interim measure, and neither is an ultimate solution that assures the availability of quality health care to all Americans. Many of the programs associated with Medicare and Medicaid are enormously wasteful because a substantial portion of the medical community has seized the opportunity offered by the new legislation's procedural inadequacies to either consciously defraud the government by submitting bogus claims, or to inflate prices by prescribing unnecessary medical tests and surgical procedures. The substitution of expensive tests for simpler, less costly procedures is a rather common occurrence; for example, prescribing a chest x-ray when an examination with stethoscope would be sufficient, a CAT Scan for an ordinary X-ray, and N.M.R. where a CAT Scan would do. Physicians are encouraged by hospitals to make use of expensive equipment and there is no personal risk to the doctor from over-prescribing medical tests. Possibly as much as fifty percent of medical treatment is unnecessary and much of that is purposefully exploitative. The medical industry, unrestrained by any regulatory authority, has vastly abused its privileged position and betrayed the American people.

The medical care industry is heavily skewed in favor of the rich and unresponsive to the needs of the poor. In 1984 Medicare and Medicaid combined pumped over $100 billion into the medical care system, Medicare primarily for treatment of the elderly and Medicaid for treatment of the poor. These funds have clearly improved the accessibility of medical care for the poor and the elderly but much more needs to be done. The use of these funds is grossly unproductive, perhaps as much as sixty to seventy percent of the funds are wasted. Both Medicare and Medicaid patients are often made to feel like lepers because the government is paying for their treatment. Medicaid patients in particular must prove not only that they are poor, but that they are impoverished and receive other forms of welfare.

Medicare and Medicaid do not reach the entire population. There are many in America who cannot afford medical insurance but who are not elderly or willing to submit to the humiliations of applying for Medicaid. The number of Americans not now covered by any form of medical insurance or a medical plan is variously estimated at between fifteen to thirty million people, the vast majority of whom are poor.

Though Medicare and Medicaid have served to extend medical care to many who would otherwise be left without it, each of these programs is in severe financial jeopardy and thus threatened by those legislators who would be quite satisfied to leave the needy without any medical attention at all.

And finally, there can be little doubt that the medical care industry gives priority to serving the needs of the rich and powerful over those of the poor and the elderly. Hospital segregation is so common that no one seems to have noticed it. The wealthy are routinely assigned to the better wings of hospitals and assigned to private or semi-private rooms; they choose from the most qualified physicians and are given numerous other preferences such as private nurses, special menus, non-standard visitation privileges, and so on. Private physicians squeeze them into otherwise tight schedules, whereas the less wealthy must often wait for weeks or months. In both out-of-hospital and in-hospital treatment money speaks with a powerful voice.

There is no precise measure of the tragic losses and suffering resulting from incompetent, impaired, and drug abusing physicians, nurses, and other health care professionals. The numerous accounts of malfeasance that appear regularly in the media are only a small part of the total. The number of malpractice suits against both physicians and hospitals has risen dramatically over the last quarter century, as has the associated cost of medical malpractice insurance, which in turn drives up medical costs. Malpractice suits occur in only a small percentage of actual malpractice cases. In the others the patient either dies without knowing that a malpractice has occurred; is convinced by associates of the physician that no malpractice occurred; is too sick or too poor to launch an appropriate complaint; or, in a majority of cases, simply does not recognize the malpractice. The disreputable expediency of one physician covering up another's malfeasance, especially in serious cases, is compounded by the fact that no public criteria exists by which a person in need of medical treatment can adequately assess the relative qualifications and competencies of prospective physicians.

The lack of information regarding the qualifications and treatment record of physicians carries over to hospitals. How is the public to evaluate the services of one hospital over another? Many major hospitals in America are plagued by uncaring staff and hospital conditions that are, ironically, more dangerous than many of the illnesses being treated. Unclean hospital conditions lead directly to patient contamination and infection. The post-operative infection rate in American hospitals is more than twice that in Canadian hospitals and growing worse each day, particularly in the large city hospitals where the gap between the incomes of physicians and non-professionals is unconscionable. Incompetent physicians work side by side with poorly paid hospital staffers, and the disparity of income, at a ratio of twenty or thirty to one, is bound to breed contention.

But perhaps the greatest abuse of medical integrity arises when, in the course of the regular practice, physicians treat illnesses that do not exist or conditions they are not qualified to treat. Patients must be protected from the multiple abuses of America's medical industry. Physicians' records should be made public and formalized procedures for their evaluation adopted. The types of illnesses a doctor is qualified to diagnose and treat should be posted in the doctor's office, along with the charges for various services and how these compare with average charges. These measures would be but a beginning of the reorganization that is needed in our medical care industry if it is to become a model for the world.

The medical industry lacks even the most fundamental self-auditing and self-correcting measures. Malpractice insurance for physicians and hospitals adds nearly $20 billion annually to the cost of medical treatment. Because physicians feel threatened by the prospect of malpractice suits, they order excessive diagnostic tests that add perhaps an additional $40 to $80 billion to the nation's annual medical treatment costs. Much of this wasteful expense is the direct result of the medical industry's lack of self-regulatory enforcement. Squalid hospitals and muddled physicians continue in business unhindered by the pandemonium they cause other doctors who are forced to co-insure their slovenly practices. There is a pervasive professional reticence about either acknowledging incompetence or promoting the establishment of regulatory agencies and rating systems within the medical profession. Both physicians and hospitals should be audited regularly for competence, quality of care, and efficiency. Ratings should be assigned each year and be published and made available to the general public. Then the public can, in turn, adequately assess their prospects for receiving quality medical care from a given hospital or physician.

Objectives

At eleven percent of GNP, the aggregate of funds flowing into the medical industry is more than sufficient for adequate health care and should be slowly reduced over time. Spending should be reduced by one-half percent a year for six years until it is no more than eight percent of GNP. With real GNP continuing to grow at least at its historical rate of two percent per annum, a decline in the percent of GNP flowing to the medical industry is not as significant as in a stagnant or declining economy.

Physician and Hospital Re-Certification

In order to contain and reduce the flow of funds to the medical industry there must be recognition that the prevailing monopolism must be discarded, that a license to practice medicine is a privilege that must be continuously renewed, and does not in and of itself bestow upon its holder an automatic right to an astronomical income. The doctor-patient relationship, presently so dominated by an artificial mystique that carries over from the days of the tribal witch doctors when pomp and ceremony were used as surrogates for actual medical knowledge, must be grounded for the first time in reality.

It is well within the patient's right to know just what medical procedures a doctor is qualified to perform, and how those qualifications measure against a certifiable standard. Further, both physicians and hospitals should be required to submit to annual certifications so that prospective incompetence, impairment, and drug abuse are nipped in the bud before they lead to malpractice and unnecessary patient suffering.

The Expansion of the Use of Non-Medical Personnel, At-Home Self-Diagnostic Testing, and Self-Prescriptions

Much of the time and energy and perhaps the majority of the cost consumed in the doctor-patient relationship is unnecessary and could be handled without the direct involvement of a physician. As regards in-hospital care, many more of the routine procedures should be turned over to the nursing staff and paraprofessionals. The enhancement of the nursing function has occurred in Canada without the development of any major problems. The main problem with the implementation of such enhancements in America would come from the medical profession's monopolistic stranglehold over the duties of the physician and the organizational disarray of our system of hospitals. In fact, once diagnosis has been made and a medical monitoring and therapy program established, there is very little that a qualified nursing staff cannot handle. Even in hospital emergency rooms, the experienced nurse is of more direct and efficient use than an unqualified or fledgling physician.

Along with the expansion of the responsibilities of non-medical personnel, the physician's monopoly over the writing of medical prescriptions should be broken. Citizens should be free to refill their own prescriptions and even to prescribe for themselves, if they so wish. To force people into the hands of unregulated and often incompetent medical practitioners is to significantly reduce their personal freedom. The general availability of illicit drugs on the streets of our nation's cities is sufficient to satisfy the suicidal desires of those who wish to abuse their bodies with unnecessary drugs.

Linked to self-prescription is self-diagnosis, a practice already quite prevalent but limited by undeveloped and badly distributed home-testing procedures, lack of symptom-oriented diagnostic literature written for at-home use, and the current monopolistic stranglehold over medical prescriptions. Much of what passes as medical practice is mere triviality because what is being treated is not serious. The medical literature should actively alert the public as to what constitutes severe or chronic symptoms and what does not. Severe and chronic medical symptoms are the appropriate domain of the medical profession; the treatment of trivial symptoms is not.

The Nation's System of Hospitals Should Be Reorganized to Reflect Advances in Medical Technology, Communications Technology, and Organizational Theory

The enormous inefficiencies that afflict the giant corporations also afflict the medical industry, and are most fully realized in the large general hospital. Instead of these behemoths, our hospital system should be reorganized into area groupings of small specialty hospitals, diagnostic centers, maternity centers, surgical centers (further divided by type of surgery), communicable disease centers, short-term and long-term care hospitals, and specifically designed emergency treatment centers. All surgical procedures and admission to long-term care hospitals would require the concurrence of at least two physicians, one representing the patient and the other the hospital or treatment center. The multi-function general hospital, together with the hodgepodge that presently constitutes our health insurance industry, does much to proliferate unproductive and expensive bureaucracy. Medical industry reorganization will both improve patient care and reduce the size of the medical bureaucracy at hospitals, while **Metacapitalism's** Guaranteed Medical Care Plan will reduce the size of the medical insurance bureaucracy and clerical requirements at the offices of individual medical practitioners.

Conclusion

Along with our much heralded political freedoms, every American is entitled to a full range of quality medical services, regardless of his or her financial standing with the American economic system. **Metacapitalism's** approach to reforming the medical industry is that all medical services should be available to each citizen free of charge, except for a $1,000 annual payment for each audit that would be charged against their Productivity Dividend. The $1,000 charge is merely to thwart the potential self-indulgences of hypochondriacs. Essentially people are free to choose between public or private health care. Private health care allows one to select the physician of one's choice and to remit to the government the full amount charged by the physician or hospital for the services rendered.

With MCA individual physicians and hospitals may derive no more than fifty percent of their revenue from private patients; that is, those who have opted to reimburse the government for their medical services as opposed to those funded by GMC. Thus, each hospital and physician must engage in the delivery of MCA services, and all payments for medical and hospital care will be channeled through the government, so as to ensure that preferential treatment does not corrupt the system. No hospital, public or private, or physician may receive payment from any patient. Instead, the hospital or physician will submit a daily account of services performed to a regional medical payment processing center, which will remit payment within one week of receipt of the daily accounting. Questionable items will be resolved within a two-week time frame. Violators of the provisions of GMC, those who overcharge or who accept cash from patients, will be censured, fined, and face the loss of their medical license.

Hospital and physician reimbursement under MCA for public patients will be a function of experience ratings which will be updated each year based on actual practice and the results of a competence audit. Chronically negligent medical practitioners will be subject to suspension and loss of license.

MCA seeks to restore sanity and fairness to the medical industry, sanity by opening it up to public scrutiny and fairness by assuring every American access to quality health care. If certain segments of the medical industry must maintain their monopolistic characteristics, then these should be controlled so that runaway medical costs inspired by greedy hospitals and physicians never again reach today's proportions, accounting for eleven percent of our nation's GNP.

THE ECONOMIC PLANNING ACT (EPA)

Introduction

The Economic Planning Act establishes an agency of the federal government as America's primary source of economic planning, and it defines, in preliminary fashion, the scope and method of economic planning.

Background

In America today there is no purposeful central economic planning or formalized industrial policy or strategy. The federal government (primarily the Federal Reserve System) intervenes with short-term monetary medicine when business cycles appear distorted, and the federal budget and the tax system are used as a device to stimulate or dampen consumer demand. But none of these short-term panaceas for a sickly economy serve as an appropriate substitute for long-term economic policy, strategy, and planning.

If America's advanced industrial society is to move beyond its current stage of uncertain capitalism, the federal government must assume a far greater role in planning and managing various components of the macroeconomy. We have seen over and over again that in times of economic crises only directed governmental action produces positive results. The Great Depression worsened as long as government remained an idle spectator. The stagflation (inflation and unemployment rising concurrently) that had beset our economy in the late 1970s and early 1980s was finally dampened, not by accident, but by directed government economic actions. Yet, there remains a great fear about developing a purposeful or deliberate attitude toward economic planning and economic management at the federal level.

The distrust of governmental economic activity emanates from many sources but always manages to avoid confronting the reality that government is already quite active in the macro-economy. Federal spending including transfer payments is approximately one-fourth of GNP. Without it, our economy would quickly deteriorate. The federal government is our sole source of domestic currency and plays a central role (through the Federal Reserve System) in managing the nation's entire supply of money. Economic growth, interest rates, credit, inflation, employment, entire industries, and even America's industrial competitiveness are all heavily influenced by both the purposeful and inadvertent actions of the federal government.

Objectives

The reasons for American government's abstention from central economic planning are partly historical, partly ideological, partly accidental, and partly the manifestation of the desires of the guardians of the status quo.

Historically, Americans have feared the various forms of persecution that ensue from unrestrained governmental power. Ideologically, some Americans have opposed central economic planning for fear it would spread public sector authority to the private sector, leading to governmental control of business (a form of creeping socialism), or worse, to the Soviet form of economic totalitarianism. At the same time, uncertain capitalism has traditionally been successful, before ways or means for planning had evolved, the rampant amateurism that tends to characterize the American political personality propelled our early government into flamboyant victories. Though political considerations tended to the short-term, accomplishments were immediately displayed as marks of achievement to the American electorate. In this way, America has been able to avoid central economic planning while *seeming* to stay above water. But it is time to point out that our government's prolonged avoidance of central economic planning works to the advantage, and is therefore currently perpetuated by, the coalition of America's monopolists and conservatives. The monopolists know full well that planning sheds light on dark places and that the aggressively restrictive and exploitative practices of the monopolists operate far better in the dark. Brainwashed conservatives have been propagandized into believing that planning is anathema to capitalism, and that planning will somehow destroy free market initiative and incentive. Moreover, these conservatives fear that dramatic central planning will tend to reduce the economic stranglehold of the monopolists and narrow the gap between rich and poor.

The conservative-monopolist coalition, with great contempt for the majority of Americans, seeks to reduce America's entire middle income group to conditions of impoverished servitude. The conservative political strategy nurtures economic monopolism at every turn. The monopolists and the conservatives are peas in the same pod. They are the old aristocracy in new clothes. Whereas **Metacapitalism** seeks to spread prosperity and economic security to all Americans, the conservative coalition with the monopolists seeks to return America to the days of lord and serf, or worse, to the days of master and slave.

J. M. Keynes wrote eloquently of the benefits of short-term central economic planning: "I believe that the cure for these things [business cycles] is partly to be sought in the deliberate control of currency and of credit by a central institution, and partly in the collection and dissemination on a great scale of data relating to the business situation . . . . These measures would involve society in exercising directive intelligence through some appropriate organ or action over many of the inner intricacies of private business, yet it would leave private initiative and enterprise unhindered." Writing in *The End of*

Laissez-Faire, Keynes said that many of the economic horrors that result from recession and depression could be mitigated by purposeful governmental economic action, specifically the gathering and dissemination of economic data, and the control of currency and credit by a central institution.

Today, all free world advanced industrial economies have adopted such Keynesian measures to mitigate the effects of business cycles. Most, as a natural corollary of short-term planning, have begun to experiment with long-term planning. As America lags behind in the evolution of citizen-directed democracy, so does it trail the rest of the free world in experimentation with central long-term economic planning. The conservative-monopolist coalition has abused short-term economic planning and turned it into a means for protecting entrenched wealth and increasing the number of impoverished Americans. This is no condemnation of short-term planning in itself, only its current practitioners. Even the best of tools may be used for evil purposes.

Short-term planning, though abused of late, has served to mitigate some of the economic horrors of business cycles. But short-term planning is not enough to implement **Metacapitalism.** Short-term planning leads naturally to longer-term considerations, to long-term economic policy and strategy and thus to long-term central economic planning. The critical question is what sort of policy, what sort of strategy, and what sort of planning?

It is possible for a nation to function with only a *de facto* economic policy. American economic policy has

213

allowed the monopolists to further their cause, taking advantage of the vacuum created by the absence of a national economic policy.

In Scandinavia economic policy promotes a mixed economy, with government controlling both the monopolies and an extensive private sector of small and medium sized businesses and farms. In France, until the relatively recent ascent of the Socialist Party, the existing economic policy favored monopolism, with the government actually providing rewards and incentives to those firms that conformed to governmental standards of market conduct, and in particular to those who furthered the cause of economic concentration. The elitist French establishment, which had been responsible for conceiving and implementing this policy of economic concentration, mistakenly popularized the incorrect notion that large or giant firms are more efficient than smaller firms. This myth has run rampant through classical economic literature since the days of Adam Smith. The theory that benefits would accrue from the specialization of function has been formalized into economic dogma. Yet whatever the special or hypothetical case, in the real world small and medium sized firms consistently outperform their large and giant counterparts.

As we have already seen, the economic monopolists have led American capitalism into a long period of uncertainty, producing prolonged economic stagnation for American workers. More than just retracting the spread of economic prosperity, such steps have severely retarded social progress. To reverse these insidious trends, the

American electorate must now direct its representatives to denounce the *de facto* policy of economic monopolism and replace it with a formalized economic policy that favors small and medium sized businesses and farms. There exists no technological impediment to the implementation of an economic policy directed at the gradual phasing out of monopolies in America. The lowering of long-distance telephone rates and the proliferation of new telephone equipment are examples of the immediate economic gains that accrue to the majority of Americans when monopolies are compelled to compete. **Metacapitalism's** Corporate Reform Act and Financial Reform Act will induce a reduction of economic concentration. The Prosperity Revenue Act will accelerate the competitive process in such a way that the monopolists will lose the privileged positions they now hold over small and medium sized firms. And the National Capital Act will provide the much needed revenue for new business and farm formation, and for the further capitalization of existing small and medium sized businesses and farms.

As regards an economic strategy for America, **Metacapitalism** seeks to reverse the special interest orientation that currently dominates American industry, domestic affairs, and international transactions. If one firm or one industry is protected, then all should be protected; not just the corporations, but farms and individuals as well. The mere thought of extending such protections to all businesses, farms, and individuals demonstrates just how ridiculous protectionist strategies are. When the American economy reaches the level it has today, where it is possible to extend economic security to the entire population, as with **Metacapitalism's** proposed Income Security Act, it is a social disgrace not to do so. But to protect industry is to dampen industriousness and make a sham of notions such as free market competition. American entrepreneurs, workers, executives, and managers must take their place with their counterparts from other nations, free and totalitarian, without special governmental protection. If other nations opt for protective measures, let them. Such protection only serves to make industry sloppy and flabby. Every industry in America now so protected falls into this category.

As for central economic planning, matters are far more elaborate. America has far less experience with central economic planning than with economic policy or strategy formation. Most people envision central economic planning in the limited spectrum ranging from Soviet authoritarianism on the extreme left to the hands off, unplanned scenario favored by the neurotic conservatives of the extreme right. Actually, when push comes to shove, or when the conservatives find their own affairs jeopardized by competition, they are the first to cry for government protection, for government intervention, for just about anything they can get in the form of special interest considerations from government. The nature of the neurotic conservative is to espouse one thing and to do the opposite. For example, who else crys out louder against governmental assistance for the unfortunate, calling it a dole that only saps initiative while at the same time passing huge sums to their children as unearned inheritances? Conservatives are constantly at battle in federal and state courts in relentless pursuit of governmental special considerations, and the costs are, unfairly, financed by the American people through their income tax.

America now sits somewhere between this extreme left and right; the federal government is involved in schemes to pick those industries which are somehow destined to be our winners and to favor them with governmental largess. Such schemes are typically called "Industrial Policy," but just how our government would go about selecting the "winners," or why government should do this is not clear. No one, and certainly no government, can foresee the future. Who could have predicted the aggressive OPEC pricing policies that precipitated the international oil crises? Who could have predicted the demise, and then the rebound, of the American automobile industry? And who can predict accurately what the future holds for the American automobile industry; or, for that matter, for the computer industry, for textiles, for steel, and so on? An "Industrial Policy" based on industrial forecasts only serves to create the realities it predicts. By subsidizing or favoring one industry over another it creates the "winner" rather than selecting the "winner."

But economic planning can play an effective, positive role in freeing markets and pricing from the abuses of the economic monopolies. Governmental management of the macro-economy within an ideological framework that favors small enterprise and the spread of prosperity, and free market competition, need not interfere with or meddle in private sector decision making to the extent it does today. Much governmental interventionism in today's marketplace results from the need to check the unbridled activities of the economic monopolies, to rescue them from their labor problems, to protect them from foreign competition, to supervise their financial manipulations, to restrain their pollutants and dangerous products, to provide legal resources for their numerous lawsuits, and occasionally to prosecute them for contract fraud, price fixing, bribery, collusion, anti-competitive mergers, and the like. Economic planning of the macroeconomy should not offer incentives to particular industries or firms (sometimes called picking the "winners" and the "losers) because such actions would serve to distort free market mechanisms, thus adversely affecting the general interests of all Americans.

Nothing that has yet been offered as a prospective "Industrial Policy" for America is consistent with the idea of freedom inherent in capitalism, nor germane to the long-term problems faced by our citizens and our economy. What is needed in America is not a meddlesome scheme that usurps already rusting market mechanisms, but rather a central economic planning vehicle that provokes competition, thwarts obstructionist tendencies, promotes the general interests of all Americans, and encourages new economic development. In short, we need central planning that capitalizes on the strengths of capitalism and reduces its weaknesses.

The intent of EPA is to formalize the role of government in our nation's economic affairs. By specifying the actions government will and will not undertake in the management of public and private sectors, economic development will be nurtured and prosperity will spread. Here it is only possible to speculate about the specific sorts of activities that would evolve from such legislation, for it is the electorate who must provide the necessary impetus and direction. *Will* a majority of Americans opt for the flat tax proposal contained in PRA or some modification of it? *Will* they opt for the Productivity Dividend set forth in ISA? *Will* Americans favor economic policies that promote new business formation and check the advance of economic monopolism? *Will* Americans favor placing a cap of five percent on interest rates and an upper limit on inheritance? These questions and many more like them must first be put to the American electorate before a meaningful EPA can be fleshed out.

There are certain guidelines, however, that should be followed. To establish a non-intrusive central economic planning activity in America requires *first* the prohibition of all governmental intervention in the private sector, unlike the current policy of "picking the winners." *Second*, it requires that America adopt a formal economic policy and strategy, based on the expressed desires of the electorate. **Metacapitalism** has proposed that the policy favor small enterprise over monopolies and adopt a strategy that features economic humanism or economic development with the intent of spreading economic security and improving the quality of life of all Americans. *Third,* it must be understood that planning has more to do with creating than predicting the future. Within this context, economic strategic planning deals with establishing societal objectives that are economically based and voter approved. For example, the desired annual rate of increase in the National Productivity Dividend or the percent of GNP to be allocated to new enterprise capitalization by the National Capital Act would be determined by the citizenry based on long-range social goals. Within this context, long-range planning would deal with the formulation of appropriate "means" to achieve the "ends" posited by strategic economic planning. Both ends and means would be presented to the American electorate for their approval, essentially creating a citizen-directed democracy as elaborated in the Voting Powers Act. *Fourth,* adequate planning requires that the Central Economic Planning Agency (CEPA) should be more depoliticized than the present Federal Reserve System. It should include the current functions of that system and of other governmental units that relate to economic affairs; parts of the Treasury Department, the Justice Department (particularly those areas dealing with antitrust enforcement), the Securities and Exchange Commission, the Federal Trade Commission, and the like. The senior council of CEPA would consist of Presidential and senatorial appointees, as well as members chosen by the general electorate, much the same as in the modifications proposed in the Political Reform Act for selecting Justices for the Supreme Court. CEPA members would select their own chief annually. *Fifth,* all

CEPA business, methodologies, policies, procedures, deliberations, memoranda, should be made public and subjected to the scrutiny of the press. In a word borrowed from those who follow the deliberations of the Scandinavian governments, planning should be conducted in a "fishbowl."

Responsibilities of CEPA should be:

1. To formulate specific economic proposals for submission to the American electorate. Were CEPA currently in existence, the Prosperity Revenue Act, the Income Security Act, the National Education Act, the Medical Reform Act, the Corporate Reform Act, the Financial Reform Act, the Community Participation Act, the National Capital Act, and, in fact, many of *Metacapitalism's* proposals would be appropriate grist for CEPA's mill.

2. To put teeth into the enforcement of economic law by prosecuting violations of antitrust and usury laws.

3. To periodically report on strengths and weaknesses within the economy, including the publication of aggregate economic data on a far more timely basis than at present. The CEPA would discuss requirements for new or modernized national infrastructure (ports, roads, institutions, and the like), and establish and report on a series of data relating to tracking the quality of life in America, such as poverty, crime, education, pollution, and mortality rates.

4. To report on government intentions in regard to budgetary allocations, the supply of money and credit, payment of the National Productivity Dividend, infrastructure improvements, and so forth.

5. To continue and improve upon the short-term planning now used to mitigate against severe business cycle fluctuations; actions such as expanding or contracting the supply of money and credit, conducting open market operations, and recommending budgetary increases or decreases.

A recently released governmental report indicates that forty percent of Americans living in poverty are children, and that the rate is increasing daily. This social disgrace is the direct result of the economic myths and discriminatory practices that dominate our land, and which have been pushed to their limits by the unconscionable guardians of the status quo. America's economic problems are homegrown, endemic, and indigenous. They result predominantly from the insufficiencies that permeate our economic ideology; an atavistic assortment of assumptions, doctrines, and programs that are appropriate to a much earlier period in our economic history than to today. Early American society was largely agrarian with a small but rapidly developing industrial base. The population was only modestly interconnected, living solitary existences, mostly self-sufficient. Today, the evening of the twentieth century, we are primarily an advanced industrial society, our individual existences highly intertwined, our dependencies highly evolved and rapidly growing. Few among us are entirely self-sufficient. Our thoroughly archaic economic ideology was earlier labeled uncertain capitalism. It is a capitalism tarnished by an entrenched and growing base of poverty; by uneven economic growth, an uncertain economic future, and a financially insecure citizenry, by enormous concentrations of wealth co-existing with destitution and deprivation, by a deteriorating physical infrastructure and inadequate housing, by a large and growing base of unsatisfactory employment and unemployment, by an increasing rate of failure among small businesses and farms, by diminished labor productivity, stagnant wages, and slippage in our standard of living, by declining competitiveness, an increased vulnerability to internal and external economic shocks, and by an inability to grow and spread economic prosperity as an answer to the Soviet economic challenge.

These are among the most important of the many economic problems that confront us. The causes of these problems are many and varied, but all are directly traceable to inattention, intransigence, mischief, mismanagement, misguidance, misconduct, and misrule on the part of our federal government. On the federal level, a preoccupation with special interests, with the property rights of the wealthy, and a pronounced amateurish approach to governance exist. Again, it was the French philosopher Diderot who said, "We have made a labyrinth and got lost in it." An organization such as CEPA will help us find our way out.

THE NATIONAL CAPITAL ACT (NCA)

In the same way that the National Education Act (NEA) provides funds to qualified students for higher education and vocational training, the National Capital Act would provide significant funding to small enterprises, businesses, and farms. The formation of new businesses and small enterprises are the sustaining forces of American capitalism. As we have seen, it is the small enterprise that is efficient and entrepreneurial, that opens new markets, creates new products, and creates new employment.

On the other hand, the giant corporations, the monopolies, pursue restrictive economic development policies. They export employment, they strangle entrepreneurial initiative, restrain competition, lobby the Congress for special interest considerations, engage in a multitude of corrupt practices in search of what is ultimately impossible—the perpetual increase of sales and profits. When a small enterprise establishes, against considerable odds, a significant market position for its product or products, the monopolists go to considerable lengths and spend considerable funds, to devour it.

America's economic monopolists presently have only two strengths that small enterprises have great difficulty countering. The monopolists have been engaged in forming a partnership with government, a partnership that yields significant capital flows from government to the giant corporations, that provides exclusive contracting, that has government look the other way when the giants violate our antitrust and other laws, that facilitates the movement of corporate executives into government policy-making positions, and the movement of high government officials into lucrative corporate positions. Government, without the consent of the electorate, has done all of this and much more. The tax laws favor the economic monopolists, who frequently pocket annual profits of hundreds of millions, even billions of dollars without paying a dime of federal income tax. With greater and greater frequency, the government steps in to rescue ailing corporate giants. And the government passes many pieces of legislation and constructs elaborate regulations, all of which serve to protect the market interests of the monopolists and restrain competition and free trade.

The partnership between government and the economic monopolists has covertly developed to such a degree that it is fair to characterize it as the *de facto* socialization of business by government. Marx would never have dreamed that the capitalism he so loathed would be transformed into an insidious socialism by a partnership between the economic monopolies and government.

225

It is the intention of **Metacapitalism** to break up the illegal partnership between the economic monopolists and the federal government. The Economic Planning Act puts forth an economic policy and strategy that favors small enterprise over economic monopolism. The Corporate Reform Act will thwart the ungainly and dangerous growth of monopolies. But, still more is needed, specifically the establishment of a continuously replenished pool of capital to aid the formation and economic development of small enterprise.

In hand capital, and the ability to raise almost unlimited funds are the other advantages the monopolies have over the small enterprise. Small business entrepreneurs are frequently forced to grovel in the dirt for even scraps of capital, while the monopolies raise billions at the drop of a hat. NCA proposes that 2.5 percent of GNP be allocated from the general tax revenue for the capitalization of small businesses and farms. The procedural and administrative aspects of NCA could be developed and managed by a National Capital Board, which, in turn, would draw heavily on the experience of the Departments of Agriculture and Commerce, and the Small Business Administration.

It is the announced intention of the Reagan Administration to phase out the Small Business Administration, which currently provides modest sums in the form of loans to small businesses. In 1984 SBA was funded with a skimpy $300 million, and is scheduled to get an increase to $700 million in 1985, and then drop to $100 million in 1986, and close down in 1987. These sums are indeed puny when considered in light of the capital needs of the nation's millions of small businesses and farms, and the hundreds of billions raised by the economic monopolists. By way of contrast, NCA would allocate to the National Capital Board 2.5 percent of GNP, which according to the current Administration's economic forecasts, would result in funding of $107.5 billion in 1986. This $107.5 billion will provide a significant impetus to the nation's small enterprises, put teeth into an economic strategy that favors small enterprise over monopolies, and produce a vibrant American capitalism for decades to come.

THE CORPORATE REFORM ACT (CRA)

Introduction

America's various antitrust laws were created in recognition of the fact that if industrial or commercial competition is unchecked, the ultimate outcome is a single or several firms that control the nation's entire stock of productive assets. Such a result would lead quite naturally to a totalitarian state, not unlike the Soviet Union, where there is, to all intents and purposes, one single firm, the Soviet state.

Background

Many myths surround the giant corporations, the economic monopolies which dominate the business and economic press and which have captured the investment community. The essence of these myths is contained in that now famous statement by a former chairman of the

228

General Motors Corporation, who in response to a governmental request, informed the government that "What is good for General Motors is good for the country." Of course, nothing could be further from the truth. The giant corporations have seriously retarded our nation's industrial and social development, produced conditions that leave us uncompetitive in the international marketplace, fostered litigiousness within society, polluted our environment and made it ugly, corrupted government processes and officials, thwarted technological development, been exploitative and imperialistic both at home and abroad, and worked against the spread of economic prosperity and economic security for all Americans.

Many myopic economists, captivated by the productive advance of capitalism over feudalism, have helped develop and perpetuate the myth that large is good. They have repeatedly tutored us about efficiencies of scale, productivity gains from the specialization of labor, and the remarkable attributes of pyramidal management. But, in advancing the case of industrial giantism these economists have forgotten to examine the long-term implications of their teachings. They have forgotten that everything in nature has an inherent limit that serves to inhibit further growth and that these limits hold for both natural and man-made creations. Every species of fauna and flora is affected, controlled, by genetic codes that prescribe the limits of its size.

Just about everything that we have been taught about the benefits of corporate giantism is wrong. Beyond the point of optimum growth, further growth is detrimental to American society. The economic monopolies do not create jobs; they restrict job creation. They are not models of efficiency; they are overly bureaucratized behemoths, and their obesity leads directly to inflexibility and lower and lower rates of productivity. It is a competitive embarrassment that American industry seeks protection from foreign competition and produces many products of vastly inferior quality. Even their profitability is a pure myth. Small and medium size businesses are far more profitable than the economic monopolies.

Our nation's farms seem to present a special case. Here, the farming monopolies seem on the face of it to outproduce the small farms. The fact of the matter is that biological and technological advances, combined with regressive governmental policies and corporate monopolism, have transformed the nature of farming from a low capital enterprise into a capital intensive business. Millions of small farmers were just not prepared for this onslaught and were left unprotected from bankruptcy.

America's giant corporate and farming monopolies are a reincarnation of feudalism; they restrict output and retard economic development, security, and the spread of social justice. They have successfully, but with significant negative impact for a majority of Americans, transformed the relatively free economics of the marketplace into a rigged game. More than a few giants have been convicted of anti-competitive practices, from price fixing and bribery to stock manipulation and monopolistic mergers in restraint of trade. The giants regularly withhold new products from the market because of established positions with old products. Their competitive sloth has transformed American industry from a world leader into a laughingstock. It is only when the giants move or fail that regional unemployment becomes a major factor. It is the giants' quest for ever-increasing profits that has led to the dangerous pollution of our air, land, and water. Those in charge are neither entrepreneurs or innovators. They are paid executives who will do almost anything imaginable to assure their own financial well-being, without regard for their employees, for the general interests of Americans, or for America herself.

Obstacles

The Antitrust Division of the Department of Justice has primary responsibility for enforcing our nation's antitrust laws. But three factors inhibit and impede their work. First, the legal system in America was created by the rich and current law is insufficient to cope with the current practices of the corporations they own. Second, the two primary acts, the Sherman Antitrust Act of 1890 and the Clayton Act of 1914 come under different jurisdictions of the federal government. Authority for enforcing the Sherman Act is vested in the Antitrust Division, one of six divisions of the Department of Justice. Supervision of the provisions of the Clayton Act is vested in the Federal Trade Commission. Such unnatural dividing of responsibility only dilutes our antitrust laws by diffusing and dispersing responsibility for their oversight and enforcement between two totally separate federal agencies. Antitrust legislation must not only be enlarged to make the punishment fit the crime by closing down those companies that flaunt the law or imposing very strict fines, it must be used to federally charter the large corporations and make them stick to the businesses for which they were chartered, and it must provide a maximum size for each type of business. The responsibility for oversight and enforcement should be merged into a single unit and that unit should be the Internal Revenue Service; the only agency that has the necessary data and means to enforce the legislation.

The allocation of the enforcement of our antitrust laws to the Internal Revenue Service will avoid one other important problem. Today, the Department of Justice is a highly politicized body. The head of that department, the Attorney General of the United States, is a cabinet level appointee and serves at the will of the President. Thus, the prioritization of the Department's working agenda is heavily influenced by Presidential politics. This being the case, and taking into account the favorable attitude of most of our Presidents toward big business, it is easy to understand why our nation's antitrust laws have all but been ignored.

Objectives

Metacapitalism's proposed Corporate Reform Act could also be called a free market restoration initiative. Almost everything sought in the act is aimed at the reduction of economic monopolism and its associated evils, and the restoration of free markets, infused with large numbers of small businesses and farms. America must rid itself of the stultifying reign of the industrial and financial giants, which, if left unchecked will almost certainly result in totalitarian rule, a distinct social retrogression.

To start, America's existing antitrust laws must be aggressively modernized, recast from the perspective that size alone is sufficiently monopolistic to require governmental action. The sheer weight of the economic power now concentrated in the first tier of America's industrial and financial institutions is an economic drag, and should no longer be tolerated. The giant organizations make a mockery of competition and free markets, even when they are not directly violating our nation's laws. The corner grocery, the luncheonette, the family farm, and every other small business is continuously threatened by the economic might of the giants. The giants make error after error but, because of a success far back in history, their business perpetuates itself. Monopolistic profits from one sector of the giant enterprise are routinely allocated to new ventures. The individual entrepreneur must face these behemoths with limited resources and without recourse to governmental bailouts, as in the recent cases of Continental Illinois, Chrysler, and Lockheed.

Conclusion

Modernization of our antitrust laws must include federal chartering, limitations on size and product mix, stiff civil and criminal penalties for antitrust abuses (including environmental abuses), restriction on corporate lawsuits, particularly corporate suits against individuals or much smaller corporations, and possibly the imposition of limited instead of unlimited life. A prospering American economy in the twenty-first century is unlikely without such modernization and its strict enforcement. We must work to free ourselves from the chains of economic monopolism now, before the predatory practices of the corporate giants have so weakened us that action is no longer possible.

THE FINANCIAL REFORM ACT (FRA)

The Financial Reform Act is primarily concerned with the inner workings of America's advanced industrial economy—the money supply, the deficit, interest rates, commercial banking, and financial speculation. The important external aspects of America's economy have been dealt with in other parts of *Metacapitalism's* proposed legislative initiative. The Corporate Reform Act deals with economic monopolism by placing restrictions on corporate growth and activity, as well as putting teeth into antitrust enforcement. The Prosperity Revenue Act, the Income Security Act, the Economic Planning Act, the National Capital Act, and the Community Participation Act all deal with economic policy and strategy, employment and income security, with investment, industriousness, productivity, and competitiveness.

From *Metacapitalism's* perspective, a nation's money supply is as critical to production and distribution in an advanced industrial society as are labor, machinery, natural resources, managerial effectiveness, and technology. The fact that the federal government has a monopoly in coining currency does not extend to the entirety of the money supply. The pervasiveness of credit enables numerous other financial institutions to create money. When a commercial bank makes loans in excess of its deposits, based on our current fractional reserve system, it is creating money.

The amount of money in supply at any one time is influenced by the policies and practices of our Federal Reserve System. If the Federal Reserve feels that the economy is overheating, it will reduce the commercial banking systems' ability to create money by conducting open market operations, raising interest rates, admonishing the bankers to desist, and the like. Essentially, what the Federal Reserve is doing is reducing the reserves available to the commercial banks for establishing the amount they may loan out at any one time. If it is felt that the economy needs stimulation, the Federal Reserve will make the opposite moves—it will lower the interest rates it charges its member banks, sell government securities, admonish the commercial bankers to lower their interest rates, and so on.

Economists, bankers, and many concerned citizens have for decades been engaged in a debate over our nation's money supply and how it is managed. From time to time, those who favor an expansive monetary policy control this debate. At other times those who favor restrictive monetary policy are at the helm. And at times those who are in control favor an even course, between expansionist and restrictive policies, with a steady growth of three or four percent.

Metacapitalism favors a fixed monetary policy: one that promotes economic growth and is pegged to production and distribution. Those who usually manage the nation's money supply are more interested in maintaining the status quo than in spreading economic prosperity. They fear extended economic growth because too much of that growth accrues to the working classes, thus closing the gap between rich and poor. They also fear extended economic contractions because these ravage even the wealthy.

Metacapitalism favors a fixed monetary policy. Any miscalculations in setting the rate of growth should err on the side of favoring expansion rather than contraction. More specifically, the quantity of money should be such that a greater quantity would not favor the financial interests of a majority of Americans while a lesser quantity would reduce the current and future production and distribution of goods and services.

Currently, interest rates are a major factor in the inner workings of the American economy. The rate of interest is used by the Federal Reserve to control the supply of money, and has thus become bound to it. The raising of interest rates slackens the demand for money in the form of loans, thus serving to reduce production and economic expansion. Another result of raising interest rates is that holders of idle monetary capital receive a greater return for the use of their capital. Possessors of idle monetary balances seek payment in the form of interest for their temporary transfer to productive pursuits. Interest income enables the idle rich to purchase goods and services without working and without depleting their capital base. But the wealthy are caught in a paradoxical situation. Most wealth is not held in the form of idle monetary balances. The value of land, common stock, natural resources, and the like tends to be greater in a vibrant economy where interest rates are low. On balance, except for those few who hold the majority of their wealth in the form of idle monetary balances, everyone benefits from low interest rates and a vibrant economy.

In America, in the mid-1980s, the citizenry is saddled with vast interest payments on the national debt, the result of mismanagement of the federal deficit. Those interest payments for the nearly 80 million Americans who pay income taxes are nearing the $175 billion level averaging more than $2,000 a year for each taxpayer. If the several hundred billion dollar a year federal deficits continue throughout the last half of the 1980s, as the Department of Commerce forecasts, by 1990 each American taxpayer will be paying an average of $4,000 to $6,000 a year just to defray the interest on the federal debt.

Background

No one knows for certain just when the practice of the payment of interest began. Economic historians have traced it back to the Byzantine Empire (395-1453 A.D.), an era characterized as politically complex and devious. At least from the time of the Byzantine Empire, possibly even earlier, the promise of interest payments has been used to induce the possessors of capital to lend their money to those who would deploy it for productive purposes, earning enough from their efforts to pay the periodic interest and ultimately repay the capital, now called principal. Throughout these 1600 years there have been numerous laws, governmental and religious, regulating the rates at which interest could be legally charged. Professional lenders of money were called usurers, a term which is now used to describe the exacting of excess or illegally high interest payments.

Two passages from the writings of the ancients amply portray official religious and governmental attitudes toward the charging of interest throughout most of history:

"From him, it says there, demand usury, whom you rightly desire to harm, against whom weapons are lawfully carried. Upon him usury is legally imposed. On him whom you cannot easily conquer in war, you can quickly take vengeance with the hundredth. From him exact usury whom it would not be a crime to kill. He fights without a weapon who demands usury: he who revenges himself upon an enemy, who is an interest collector from his foe, fights without a sword. Therefore, where there is the right of war, there is also the right of usury."

"A true friend not only takes no usance on a loan—indeed, the loan (mutuum) is an occasion for the expression of charity and brotherly love—but even waives his legal right to exact the penalty if the debtor break. The true friend shows human gentleness and love; sympathizes with the debtor, compelled to break an act of God;

loses the forfeiture, nay more, forgives a moiety of the principal, glancing an eye of pity on his losses. Only the enemy, who cannot be expected to entertain such scruples, let alone exercise such charity, may exact the penalty with better face."

The exacting of interest was alternately frowned upon and sanctioned by officialdom, but even when considered most vile, the rate of interest did not usually exceed six percent. In fact, throughout its recorded history, at least until recently, interest rates have fluctuated in the narrow range of one percent to six percent, perhaps averaging three percent to four percent. The astronomical interest rates experienced in America and much of the free world, twenty percent to thirty percent in the late 1970s and ten percent to twenty percent in the 1980s, have been until now unheard of. These greatly exaggerated costs of capital are a reflection of a world banking system, and particularly the American banking system, gone astray. These grossly excessive interest rates have worked wonders to retard economic growth and the spread of prosperity. With regard to the federal debt and the interest payments thereon, we witness no more than an outright fraud. This interest payment, paid by the taxes of 80 million Americans is in fact an unlegislated tax increase, and a particularly abhorrent one, because it represents no more than a direct transfer from the low and middle income earners to the rich.

Usury laws are not new to the United States. Each of our fifty states has enacted laws defining the maximum permissible rate of interest, usually distinguishing between rates to individuals and rates to businesses. The recently enacted federal Fair Credit Act was intended to address the predatory practices of banks and other lending institutions against unwitting individuals, euphemistically called consumers, as in consumer loans.

Individual consumers are almost always charged interest rates far in excess of those charged to businesses. The stated grounds for this prejudicial dichotomy is the supposed larger risk that obtains to the lending institution when dealing with an individual. But actual experience demonstrates precisely the opposite. It is not consumer loans that has recently brought the American banking system to the brink of collapse, but rather loans to large corporations (so-called energy loans), and loans to foreign countries. Instead of helping to promote economic growth in America, our commercial banking institutions have transformed what should be a stabilizing influence into a destabilizing one by falling victim to excessive greed and speculative fever.

To restore stability to our economy, the Fair Credit Act should be amended to eliminate the dichotomy between consumer loans and business loans. A single rate of interest should prevail, and that rate should not exceed five percent.

The extraordinarily excessive interest rates that have dominated economic activity in the 1970s and 1980s were the covert tools of the guardians of the status quo. These tools were deployed to derail the American Dream, to confuse and confound small enterprises, to redistribute financial assets from the low and middle income groups

241

to the wealthy, to sap the initiatives of underdeveloped and developing nations, and to refuel the waning energies of America's economic monopolists.

The full extent of the insidious manipulation of interest rates to accomplish the social and economic objectives of the wealthy and the powerful will in all probability never be fully known. But an examination of a new economic phenomenon, the triple digit federal deficit, effectively demonstrates how the government uses interest payments to tax the low and middle income groups in our society.

The Triple Digit Federal Deficit: The Unseen Tax Increase

The economic facts since 1982, the dawning of the era of the TDFD, work in its favor: (1) The American economy has experienced its most vigorous growth in decades; (2) Our industries appear to have regained some of their international competitiveness; (3) Inflation is controlled; (4) Interest rates are heading down; and (5) A majority of Americans profess an increased sense of well-being. If our economic stability is threatened, it would seem that the threat ensues more from the misbegotten foreign adventurism of certain of our commercial bankers than from excessive spending by government.

Nonetheless, the sheer magnitude of the TDFD engenders a terrible feeling of impending doom. Direct experience with TDFDs is of short duration. No person can be said to understand this economic phenomenon,

242

and certainly no person can forecast accurately the short, intermediate or long-term effects of current or future TDFDs with anything approaching certainty. The conventional wisdom says they need to be reduced, but prevailing policy has been to live with them, perhaps to encourage them. An understated but nevertheless remarkable fact is that the TDFD was created by an administration of self-styled fiscal conservatives, pledged to balancing the federal budget.

Single and double digit federal deficits are no new phenomenon. Our last federal surplus was a puny $3.2 billion in 1969 and before that an even smaller $.3 billion in 1960. For the thirty-six years from 1946 to 1981, the aggregate federal deficit was a mere $506 billion, an average of $14 billion a year. Even at that low rate there were more than a few fiscal conservatives who turned purple thinking about our mounting federal debt. But in 1982 what was before a trickle of federal debt became a flood which shows every sign of becoming a raging tidal wave. In just four years, from 1982 to 1985, the federal deficit will amount to over $700 billion, or $175 billion a year, which when added to the previous federal debt exceeds $1.75 trillion. Surely those fiscal conservatives who had turned purple before should have hemorrhaged by now.

Placed in perspective, the TDFD is no more than a blip on our nation's balance sheet. At the end of World War II the federal deficit was running at a rate of twenty-five percent of GNP. Now it is a mere five percent, about $2,000 a taxpayer. Surely the reason that the fiscal conservatives have not hemorrhaged is that they have discovered that the TDFD is really an unseen tax increase. The TDFD is real enough, but its reality is not as it appears. When government overspends its budget it has two choices. It can monetarize the debt, pay it off by printing new money, or pay it off by borrowing money already in existence. Monetarization is devaluation by another name and it impacts entrenched wealth negatively, so our government usually borrows old money instead of printing new money to pay its debts.

When government borrows, it borrows from the wealthy because only the wealthy have money to lend. In return for their loans, the government pays the wealthy a handsome rate of interest. The annual interest payment on $1.75 trillion is in the neighborhood of $175 billion, nearly as much as the combined expenditure for medical care and education. And where does the money to pay this rather hefty annual interest payment to the wealthy come from? From you and me. From the average American taxpayer.

Wealthy Americans benefit directly from the TDFD by receiving enormous annual interest payments. They also benefit indirectly in two ways. Much of government spending accrues to the benefit of the giant corporations in the form of production and service contracts. These corporations are owned by the wealthy, who reap dividends from the corporate giants. Beyond the dividends, the wealthy benefit still a third time when increased corporate profits from government spending increases the value of their shareholdings.

With all of these benefits accruing to the wealthy from the TDFD, it should come as no surprise that the other America has not been as fortunate. With the era of the TDFD, Americans have experienced a significant widening in the gulf between rich and poor, between the privileged and the underclasses, between vulgar consumption and massive deprivation. The real wickedness of the TDFD is considerably greater than the cruel transfer of money from working people to the wealthy. The real villainy is that the TDFD forcefully deflects attention from the real problems that afflict our society and our economy. The stagnation of wages and the growing rate of poverty are real problems. The steadily rising trend in the rate of unemployment and the over-trivialized nature of much of America's employment are real problems. The slipping standards and massive cost acceleration in our medical and educational systems are real problems. The near collapse of our commercial banking system, the inadequacies of our Social Security Fund and our current tax base are real problems. And, worst of all, our inability to mobilize our vast productive resources to feed the many millions of human beings who are now starving to death is more than a problem, it is a national disgrace.

Various plans have been offered to reduce the Triple Digit Federal Deficit. They are an ineffective litany ranging from the banal—raise taxes, cut the budget—to the ridiculous—sell government assets, start a national lottery. This rhetoric is nothing more than unproductive nonsense. Now is the time for all Americans to begin focusing on our very real social and economic problems, and not on phantoms like the TDFD. The central issue facing America today, the problem that summons forth all of the others, is that the American brand of capitalism is so fraught with irregularities and ambiguities that the forward momentum of our society is badly obstructed. The vast deterioration of our physical infrastructure deflects attention away from the unresponsiveness and general ineptness that characterizes our institutional infrastructure. If we wish to take our final approach to the twenty-first century assured of a proper course, we must stop treating our economic problems with superficial ointments and begin to address them with the recaptured vigor and courage of our revolutionary forefathers.

When, as in the 1950s and 1960s, economic security seemed to be gaining among low and middle income groups, the conservative guardians of the status quo could be counted on to invoke a vast arsenal of old and new economic weaponry to stop it. We have examined at some length the disgrace of our national system of taxation, and how it burdens income while ignoring wealth. We have seen how the Federal Reserve System manipulates the money supply and interest rates to thwart economic development, while it favors and actively encourages a two-tiered system that enriches the wealthy while it defrauds consumers, workers, and small enterprises. We have analyzed the thoroughly modern TDFD and seen that it is no more than a conservative device for using an unseen tax to transfer income to the wealthy. These, then, are some of the public sector's more important contributions the economic oppression of the vast majority of Americans.

There is another set of insidious economic weapons used to the same end. The extensive partnership between the economic monopolists and the federal government, though obnoxious and illegal, almost totally controls the nature of economic development by promoting economic concentration. Antitrust laws are ignored, property rights are elevated far above human rights, people are purposely separated from the means of production, and the capitalization of the monopolies is greatly facilitated while small enterprises are starved.

Yet another component of the inner American economy that serves to foster economic oppression among the majority of Americans is the vast network of commercial banks, financial and quasi-financial organizations, and their so-called regulatory agencies. Together these various organizations are a veritable army in the service of entrenched wealth.

To say which segment of this vast financial network is the worst offender is difficult. But a partial list of how they daily defraud a majority of Americans is in order. It was the commercial banks that pioneered a two-tiered system of interest rates. Under the system the monopolists and the wealthy receive far higher rates of interest on their deposits than the great majority of depositors. The wealthy also may borrow from the banks at rates far lower than the vast majority of borrowers. The banks set aside special people to handle the accounts of the wealthy, and even go so far as to set up special counters for them so that they do not have to wait in line with the majority of Americans. It was the credit card companies followed by the commercial banks that transformed a nation of depositors into a nation of borrowers at usurious rates, frequently as high as nineteen percent. As a whole, the predatory segment of the financial community has gone far beyond merely declaring a perpetual open season on the vast majority of Americans. A full range of banks aggressively invited farmers to borrow. Now they are eager to foreclose on their foundering farms. The large commercial banks, with their monopolistic appetites for continuous growth in revenue and profit have nearly bankrupted the American monetary system by adroitly exporting an excess of our working capital while importing defaulted foreign loans. Without foreign policy credentials of any sort, and without any mandate from the American people, or any detectable expertise, the unbridled greed of our nation's commercial bankers has wreaked financial havoc overseas and brought the international economy to the brink of depression. At home, the nation's sixth largest commercial bank, Continental Illinois, collapsed and was then salvaged by the federal government. It collapsed because of an excess of extremely poor loans to the energy industry. Many other huge commercial banks verge on failure because their foreign loans are in disarray. The case is quite clear. The American economy simply does not need private banking monopolies. The risks they run in search of ever more elusive profits for the benefit of a tiny minority of entrenched wealth daily compromise our lives unnecessarily.

Last, but certainly not least in their despicable attitudes toward hard working Americans are the numerous brokerage firms, the stock brokers and commodity brokers that dot our land. To the rich they offer quite favorable treatment, often including a monthly accounting of historical profit and loss for the account. But for low and middle income investors there is usually no such accounting, only a greedy broker churning the account for every cent it is worth. These firms function like giant pinball machines, taking a person's savings, but giving back nothing in return except for the transient thrill of the game. Not one small investor in twenty makes a decent return in the stock market, and not one in one hundred in the commodity or option markets; conversely, most see their savings diminish or completely evaporate. At a minimum, these firms should be held to account for their activities on behalf of small and medium investment accounts. And this should include financial disclosure of just how well they really do. It should be kept in mind that the man who ran the Treasury while the administration was creating the Triple Digit Federal Deficit, the unseen tax increase to low and middle income earners, is the very same man who ran the nation's largest brokerage firm, characterized by the national advertising of a stampeding herd. What the ad forgot to mention was that the object of the stampede was to crush small and medium sized investors.

THE COMMUNITY PARTICIPATION ACT (CPA)

Many Americans have an underlying malaise, a feeling that their lives lack appropriate dimension and are being wasted. Many aspects of American life are marginal or sub-marginal, begging for an application of American knowhow, but sorely lacking an appropriate institutional infrastructure, funding, and human resources. The absence of infrastructure and funding is intolerable. It is just one more manifestation of the economic strategy of the conservative-monopolist coalition that seeks a permanent division between the wealthy few and the vast majority of Americans.

The Community Participation Act is designed to bring forth, after extensive study, an appropriate institutional infrastructure and level of funding (2.5 percent of GNP is allocated in Metacapitalism's Pro Forma 1986 Federal Budget). Human resources will readily follow and the millions of opportunities to improve life that are now missed each passing day will be realized. Millions of employed and retired Americans would happily volunteer their knowledge, skills, and energies in the service of their communities, but are thwarted or discouraged from doing so because of the lack of adequate channels. Each year millions of teenagers complete their secondary educations only to pass haphazardly into the adult labor force, the military, higher education, criminal activity, or the lines of the unemployed.

As we shall see from the following breakdown, CPA would have a positive impact on the lives of all Americans. In the first group are the recent graduates of high school and those who have dropped out. For them, CPA will provide both training and a means of acclimatization into the responsibilities of adulthood. Concurrent with their training, these youths will be made available to their communities to work on a variety of useful projects. Remuneration for the participants will be provided in the form of a modest wage and, more importantly, in the form of educational vouchers that can be used to further their training. CPA will also offer high school credits to dropouts so they can obtain the diploma they so badly need.
There are many precedents in our society for this type of program. The New York City Volunteer Corps offers high school dropouts the opportunity to earn $80 a week staffing shelters for the homeless, rehabilitating city parks, and assisting at geriatric centers. The California Conservation Corps assigns youth to environmental tasks such as repairing dams, clearing salmon streams, and helping fight forest fires. The Northwest Youth Corps places pools of young workers at the disposal of private businesses for short-term work assignments like replanting forests after timber harvests.

During the Ford and Carter administrations, government funded the Comprehensive Employment and Training Act (CETA) to give young people from poor families the chance to overcome the deficiencies of training occasioned by their poverty. Unfortunately, in today's reactionary climate, CETA has been allowed to expire, and local and state programs haven't been large enough to take up the burden.

CPA, unlike CETA, would be directed at all young people and would be a mandatory service program. The mandatory aspect of the program would create a recognition on the part of youth that, as citizens in a democracy, they are responsible for its proper functioning. It would get them off the streets and reduce the crime rate while producing more socially conscious adults.

The second group favorably affected by CPA would be people who are highly dissatisfied with their present employment or are unemployable for lack of suitable training. CPA would allow them, while actively engaged in productive community service, to acquire new skills and to build upon existing skills. The newly awakened energy that derives from retraining will help boost American productivity and thus directly benefit all Americans.

The third group positively impacted by CPA will be retirees. By the year 2000, forty-five percent of all Americans will be over the age of fifty-five. Advancements in medical techniques and the new emphasis on health have increased the life span of the entire nation. A current human tragedy of immense proportion is the vast number of people now growing old and unncessarily idle; their lives are depleted and society loses their great knowledge and experience. CPA will provide a framework for the continuing productivity of the elderly and everyone will benefit.

The fourth group affected by CPA is America's vast working population. Given the changed nature of much of American employment—shorter working hours and less human toil—many people would gladly volunteer a part of their time to community programs if only an appropriate framework or institutional infrastructure existed.

Beyond the vital improvements to the quality of life for all Americans and the enhancement of the transition from youth to adulthood, there will be new outlets for Americans to use their energies in meaningful pursuits. American democracy will be strengthened by the spirit of community which is a natural derivative of community service. The alienation that now afflicts vast numbers of Americans as they stand powerless in the face of so many of our existing institutions will be significantly reduced. The participative consciousness will be greatly expanded as many stretch their personal associations beyond self and family to neighborhood, community, and nation.

The very idea of a truly participative democracy was greatly feared by our Founding Fathers. They were skeptical of unfettered democracy and placed many obstacles in its path. Our bicameral legislature, which makes a mockery of the democratic concept of one person, one vote, our representative form of government, federalism, and the electoral college are all impediments that *Metacapitalism* has sought to strip away. The Community Participation Act embodies the institutionalization of community action, gives it credence and funding, and thus greatly facilitates the transition from illusory democracy to true democracy.

THE JUDICIAL REFORM ACT (JRA)

Justices of the United States Supreme Court agree. Judges from every tier the federal, state, and local judiciaries agree. Prosecutors, federal agents, policemen, lawyers, plaintiffs, defendants agree. Everybody agrees. But, nobody seems to act. From the highest to the lowest court, from the most important to the most trivial law, from the highest security prison to the prisons without walls and the probation systems, America's edifice of jurisprudence is regarded as a confused, chaotic, and anachronistic embarrassment. Worse than that, our judicial system promotes rather than retards crime, and often rewards criminals while punishing the innocent. In all of its anachronistic aspects the system is thoroughly unjust, almost always preferring property rights over human rights. Like our taxation system, our judicial system must be subjected to intensive scrutiny and sweeping reform to make it simpler, fairer, and more efficient.

For more than two hundred years, the various Congresses and state legislatures have pieced together a crazy patchwork of criminal and civil laws that were doubtless enacted to dispense justice, but which actually accom-

255

plish quite the opposite. In the very best light, our judicial system is slow and inept. While considerable effort is expended in enforcing laws that breed more and more crime, numerous victims of violent crime, of state, corporate and individual malfeasances are left on the courthouse steps either unable to afford justice, or awaiting judicial decisions that often take years and sometimes decades.

Nothing less than a complete overhaul of our judicial system, from the United States Supreme Court down to the thousands of local traffic courts, is required. And of concern are not just the means to justice, but the very ends of justice. The innumerable procedures are necessarily confused and a burden on society. But even if they were clear and orderly, justice could not be had because justice itself is unclear and uncertain in America.

Justice in America has been fashioned by the few who are wealthy and powerful in order to sustain their property interests against encroachment by the many. Let a poor person wander across private property seeking access to the ocean and he or she may be prosecuted for trespass or even shot. But let a predatory landlord cheat hundreds or thousands of tenants and the penalty, if any, will be no more than a slap on the wrist. In America highly sophisticated corporate criminals commit grievous crimes each day and even when caught go unpunished, while children are arrested and imprisoned for stealing food. A majority of lawsuits are begun not with the intention of resolving a legitimate dispute, but rather as a form of blackmail by the rich to intimidate the poorer adversary into a settlement. Jurisdictional technicalities make a mockery of an orderly, standardized, or timely pursuit of justice. Multi-billion dollar corporations, with veritable armies of legal counsel, regularly press suit upon the poor and disabled, who are often forced to trial without benefit of legal help. Each day prosecutors commit far more grievous crimes against defendants in pursuit of convictions than the defendants themselves are charged with. Corruption runs rampant through every segment of the judicial system. Every lawyer, and there are 35,000 new lawyers in America each year, can relate numerous tales of corrupt judges and prosecutors. Federal district judges have been convicted of accepting bribes and many members of the very Congresses and state legislatures that have created our crazy patchwork of laws have themselves been convicted of accepting bribes, of corruption, collusion, and obstruction of justice. Bribery has reached right up to the Vice Presidency of the United States, and many believe that we have suffered corrupt Presidents.

The maxims that a person is innocent until proven guilty, and that justice is blind are mere shams. Once accused of a crime a person must struggle emotionally and financially to clear his or her name. The judicial system and society treats the accused as if guilt is presumed from the very fact of the charges. That justice is blind is true enough, but not in the way meant. Justice is only blind to the needs of the poor, while quite diligent in protecting the wealthy. Who has seen a contract written to favor a poor person? Our prisons are filled to overflowing with poor people while the wealthy are excused by our so-called system of justice, time after time, crime after crime.

Justice as an end in itself is not a concept much promulgated in our nation's law schools. Not energized by enlightened principles and precepts, our nation's system of jurisprudence is haunted by obsessives; obsessive judges who use it to satisfy their thirst for power, obsessive prosecutors whose win/lose ratio dominates their thinking, obsessive lawyers who use it as a means to satisfy their greed, and obsessive litigants who use it to bludgeon their adversaries into submission.

Judge Irving R. Kaufman, who has served as chief judge of the United States Court of Appeals for the Second Circuit, has correctly concluded that America desperately needs a new system of jurisprudence. Writing in the Op-Ed Section of *The New York Times* he calls for a judicial plan that will examine the ends we wish our court system to serve, and for a reordering of priorities and the choice of means by which they may be achieved. "The aim of such a plan would be to define the proper role of the judicial branch and refocus its energies. It would be foolish to ignore the lessons of history, but we would be less than courageous if we failed to consider innovative and promising measures."

Metacapitalism's proposed Judicial Reform Act would incorporate the salient features of such a plan and would demand that it be immediately undertaken. For starters the plan should seek to reduce fifty percent of the criminal and civil caseload, on the criminal side by decriminalizing victimless crimes such as drug use and prostitution, and on the civil side by freeing the courts from their role as bill collectors.

America's antidrug laws are a perfect example of how wrongheaded laws breed crime instead of preventing it. The first antidrug laws, passed in 1914, were anti-Chinese laws: certain citizens expressed alarm at the rise in opium dens that had accompanied the Chinese immigrants (overlooked were the many white middle and upper income opium addicts who regularly substituted the over the counter drug laudanum for alcohol). As more and more drugs were prohibited, their sale shifted from the drugstores and opium dens to the back alleys of the ghettos, where the desperadoes took over. The very same thing happened when alcohol was outlawed during the era of Prohibition (1920-1933). Prohibition was repealed, but the drug laws were expanded, and with that expansion the streets of America's cities have become more and more unsafe as each year millions of innocent people fall victim to muggings and other forms of robbery as drug addicts take to the streets to finance their drug habits.

The nation's drug laws have made the cost of drugs artificially high. What would cost no more than fifty cents in a drugstore costs twenty dollars or more on the street. Youths in their early teens, some even earlier, begin to experiment with drugs, not from need, but rather because the drugs are outlawed. Today, approximately ten million Americans are addicted to alcohol; the addictive personality is not easily thwarted and will usually find some means of self-degradation. The number of drug addicts in

America is far less, perhaps one million. But they account for ten times as much crime, a ratio of one hundred to one.

The back alley desperadoes of old have organized. Drug dollars account for a quite significant percentage of the revenues of organized crime, revenues that are used to finance many other criminal operations and to prey upon and purchase legitimate enterprises. Now is the time to repeal our nation's misbegotten drug laws. In terms of physical and emotional damage, studies clearly indicate that drug addiction is no more harmful than alcohol addiction. By repealing drug laws, street crime will be more than halved and $50 billion to $100 billion will be saved in law enforcement, all of which could be shifted to the National Productivity Dividend. What many have long considered unthinkable is now mandatory. Our nation's drug laws should be immediately repealed.

Many other aspects of our criminal and civil systems of jurisprudence require modernization and standardization. Sentences, fines, and judicial processes should be standardized throughout the fifty states, including all but the most local laws, which serve to set community standards. Damages should be awarded to those found innocent of criminal charges and those who lose at civil suit should bear their adversaries legal expenses. All civil cases amounting to less than $10,000 should be automatically submitted to arbitration, bypassing the courts entirely. Corporations should be precluded from suing individuals and the giant corporations should be barred from using the courts to bludgeon smaller competitors.

The procedural processes for removing incompetent judges should be made more efficient and citizen review of all criminal cases should be initiated. Those members of the justice system who initiate or are party to the initiation of criminal charges without substantial grounds should themselves be criminally charged.

The inefficiency, injustices, and incompetencies that mar our nation's system of jurisprudence are far too lengthy to report here. Certainly they are more than a match for the Grace Commission's voluminous report on governmental waste and inefficiency. Nearly half a million citizens are currently imprisoned in America, and the number grows with each passing day. A study of our nation's laws and judicial procedures, as called for by the Judicial Reform Act, must seek to reverse this insidious trend and to significantly reduce the litigiousness that has invaded our society.

THE FEDERAL BUDGET
METACAPITALISM VS. UNCERTAIN
CAPITALISM

The quality of life, life itself, for the vast majority of Americans is intimately related to domestic economic conditions. Those conditions, in turn, are related to the federal budget, which documents government's receipt of revenue and its schedule of projected outlays for the numerous projects and programs it conducts. Governmental receipts take many forms, but individual taxes, borrowing (not reflected in the government's budget as revenue, only as deficit), corporate taxes, and excise taxes account for the bulk of current governmental receipts. Social Security, which is a highly regressive payroll tax, is split almost equally between individuals and corporations and has been thus allocated. Under uncertain capitalism, governmental revenue, (and hence the federal budget, and all its outlays), are essentially a function of taxes on income. Within the current federal schema for taxation, the full burden falls on income, while wealth is all but ignored. Thus a person or a family with earnings of $20,000 or $40,000 will pay ten to twenty-five percent of their income to finance government, while a person or a family with enormous wealth, say $10 or $100 million, and no income, may enjoy life in America without paying a single cent.

Receipts are one side of the federal budget ledger. Under uncertain capitalism federal receipts are almost wholly a function of individual and corporate income, a fact which greatly favors entrenched wealth. Outlays take two forms, expenditures and transfer payments. Expenditures are governmental spending for federal employees, national defense, interest payments, and the like. Transfer payments are just that: monies collected by the federal government under its various taxing powers that are by law earmarked for particular ongoing programs, such as Social Security. Under uncertain capitalism, those outlays or transfer payments that result in direct payments to individuals account for only forty-one percent of the projected 1986 federal budget, national defense is twenty-nine percent, interest payments are fifteen percent, grants to states and localities are ten percent, and other governmental operations are five percent. Thus, under the current system far less than half of governmental outlays flow directly to the vast majority of Americans, while the bulk of federal expenditures find their way to the coffers of the wealthy. Presently, the federal budget, aided and abetted by our anachronistic system of federal taxation, is one of the most important tools of the stalwart guardians of the status quo for dividing American into a nation with a minority of rich and a majority of poor.

Economic Assumptions

In comparing the administration's projected 1986 federal budget to what would be **Metacapitalism's** projected federal budget, baseline GNP will be set in accord with administration projections at approximately $4.3 trillion. Projected GNP plays an important part in any national budgetary process, because it is from the level of economic activity that income, and thus tax revenue, is derived. Under uncertain capitalism the levels of individual and corporate income are made critically important to the funding of the federal budget because the nation's wealth is ignored in the taxation process. But under **Metacapitalism** the impact of current income on the way the federal budget affects the quality of life is greatly mitigated because governmental receipts are divided more or less evenly between those derived from income and those derived from wealth. Furthermore, under **Metacapitalism** the National Productivity Dividend may be used to stimulate economic activity; the tax on wealth provides the nation with a greatly expanded capital base. Direct transfers to individuals, states and communities, and small enterprises are far greater under **Metacapitalism** in proportion to the total budget: approximately $1.6 trillion, as opposed to $400 billion under uncertain capitalism, which is a fourfold increase.

Composition of Projected 1986
Federal Budget Receipts Under **Metacapitalism**

Metacapitalism's Prosperity Revenue Act, which would replace current federal tax law, places a roughly equal taxation burden on current income and on accumulated wealth.

• Income and social insurance taxes are combined under **Metacapitalism** (Social Security is eliminated). A flat tax of ten percent on corporate revenue and individual income will yield $350 billion and $300 billion, respectively, or $650 billion, as compared to the administration's projected $648.3 billion.

The remarkable difference is that the administration's tax receipts represent ninety-one percent of total federal revenue, whereas corporate revenue and individual income taxes represent only 30.5% of governmental revenue with **Metacapitalism.**

• Corporate and individual wealth taxed at an annual rate of five percent will yield an additional $1.25 trillion.

• State and local property taxes, currently appraised and collected on a highly decentralized basis, and grossly unfair, will raise an additional $125 billion. This will be immediately transferred back to local communities to fund secondary education based on student head counts.

• Excise taxes at $60 billion, estate and gift taxes at $30 billion, and miscellaneous receipts at $18.6 billion comprise the remainder of federal revenue receipts under

Metacapitalism's Prosperity Revenue Act, to give a total of $2.1336 trillion.

Thus under *Metacapitalism's* Prosperity Revenue Act, the total of individual income taxes would fall from $503.6 billion, as under uncertain capitalism, to approximately $300 billion, and would be further reduced by an individual's offsetting receipt of the National Productivity Dividend, which is not taxed. Corporate taxes would rise from $218.8 billion to approximately $350 billion due to the combined result of a greatly expanded tax base, the elimination of all tax deductions, and a flat ten percent tax on revenues.

Thus, from the combined individual and corporate income taxes, *Metacapitalism,* on GNP of $4.3 trillion in 1986, would raise $650 billion to the Administration's projected $724.4 billion, for a net income tax cut of nearly twelve percent, only fifteen percent of GNP, as opposed to the administration's seventeen percent. Excise tax rates would be doubled (causing spending for luxuries to fall somewhat) to raise an additional $25 billion—up from $35 billion to $60 billion. Estate and gift taxes, which have been virtually eliminated by this administration, would be raised to $30 billion, up from $5.3 billion. Miscellaneous receipts would rise from $18.6 billion to $25 billion, reflecting charges for such services as free corporate trials now given free only to the wealthy. Customs and duties would fall from $12.3 to zero because these only serve to distort free markets and impede free trade. State and local property taxes would remain at their current levels, and serve their current function, the funding of secondary education. In the interest of fairness and efficiency, responsibility for the collection of these would be transferred to the federal government, and disbursal based on student head counts in the various communities.

At this point, most similarity between the administration's projected federal budget for 1986 and *Metacapitalism's* projected federal budget for 1986 come to an abrupt end. In addition to the $890 billion already raised by *Metacapitalism* (by income and other traditional taxes and fees), the Prosperity Revenue Act proposes to raise an additional $1.25 trillion by taxing existing corporate and individual wealth at an annual rate of five percent. The true store of wealth in America is not documented with any precision. *Metacapitalism* intends to include provisions for the exclusions of household and small enterprise wealth, up to $100,000 to $250,000. By incorporating a tax on wealth, *Metacapitalism* effectively recapitalizes America, providing the wherewithal for America's transition to a just society, one that is truly humane and compassionate, one that esteems rather than defiling its weakest members.

In total, government receipts under *Metacapitalism's* federal budget in 1986 are $2.140 trillion, approximately fifty percent of GNP, and far more than the administration's projected receipts of $948.8 billion, less than twenty five percent of GNP. Even to maintain the country on its present course, the administration needs far more revenue in 1986 than it currently admits. Even if the administration continues unchecked in its program to disenfranchise poor and middle income groups, reducing an even greater percentage of America's citizenry to conditions of poverty, it will still need ten to twenty percent more tax revenue than is currently projected.

COMPARISON OF 1986 FEDERAL BUDGET OUTLAYS UNDER *METACAPITALISM* AND UNCERTAIN CAPITALISM BY FUNCTION

Here is shown how revenue raised is disbursed. Categorization by function allows for far greater brevity because only the primary purpose of each function, and not the multitude of specific programs and agencies, are discussed. Current federal budgetary procedures exclude sums for guaranteed loan commitments and direct loan obligations. *Metacapitalism's* outlay budget will highlight new loan commitments, but exclude them from the comparative figures.

The Administration's 1986 budget lists eighteen functions. Again, for the sake of brevity and clarity, five of these functions (Administration of Justice, Energy, Commerce and Housing Credits, General Government, and General Purpose Fiscal Assistance) have been combined into an 'other' category. In addition, the administration's

269

1986 FEDERAL BUDGET OUTLAYS: METACAPITALISM VS. UNCERTAIN CAPITALISM

Outlays By Function
(In billions of dollars)

Metacapitalism				*Uncertain Capitalism*		
As % of GNP	As % Budget	Budget	Category	Budget	As % Budget	As % of GNP
5.0	10.0	215.0	National Defense	285.7	29.3	6.6
1.0	2.0	43.0	International Affairs	18.3	1.9	0.4
0.5	1.0	21.5	General Science, Space, & Technology	9.3	1.0	0.2
0.5	1.0	21.5	Natural Resources & Environment	10.8	1.1	0.3
0.5	1.0	21.5	Agriculture	6.6	0.7	0.2
1.0	2.0	43.0	Transportation	25.9	2.6	0.6
2.5	5.0	107.5	Community & Regional Development	7.3	0.8	0.2
7.0	8.2[1]	301.0	Education, Training, Employment, & Social Services	29.3	3.0	0.7
7.0	14.1	301.0	Health	107.4	11.0	2.5
25.0	50.4	1075.0	Income Security	265.9	27.3	6.0
-0-	-0-	-0-	Net Interest	142.6	15.0	3.3
1.0	2.0	43.0	Other Functional Items	21.1	2.1	0.5
2.5	-0-[1]	107.5	National Capital Fund	-0-	-0-	-0-
1.1	3.1	66.6	Surplus/Deficit (Receipts less Outlays)	180.0	18.3	4.2
		Surplus		Deficit		

[1]$125 billion of the $301 billion allocated to education and the $107.5 billion National Capital Fund, are loans & thus excluded from percent of budget calculations.

270

projections for Social Security and Medicare have been allocated to Income Security and Health, as have Veterans' Benefits and Services. *Metacapitalism's* budget has added only one function, the National Capital Fund, to provide financing for small enterprises.

National Defense

The maintenance and modernization of conventional and strategic forces is made necessary by the predatory instincts and territorial aggressiveness of present and future totalitarian dictatorships. No war has ever been commenced by the direct vote of a nation's citizenry, nor would one ever be, except possibly for those of a revolutionary character, where the taking up of arms were the only way to remove an oppressive government.

The protection of the American people and our allies from invasion has been and should continue to be the foremost responsibility of government. For these reasons it is desirable to allocate vast sums to this function. Unfortunately, the large sums now expended for national defense have attracted the economic monopolists, who now dominate defense contracting and have turned it into a disgrace. Each day we read about how one or another of the monopolists has defrauded the government, and thus the American people, by criminally abusing the contracting process. The Defense Department regularly overpays for weapons systems and spare parts, while many in the military are forced to live in poverty. An Army private, with a wife and child, earns approximately $950 a month in pretax income, while the Department of Defense spends:

$170.98 for a $26.99 flashlight
$13,905 for a crew chief's chair
$74,165 for an aluminum ladder
$17.69 for a $.69 bolt
$166,097 for engine doors
$7,622 for a coffee maker
$670.06 for aircraft armrests
$436.00 for a $7.00 hammer
$659.00 each for ashtrays
$1,118 for plastic stool-leg caps
$16,571 for single refrigerators
$400.00 for a socket wrench

Each of these examples is small potatoes compared to the exploits of several major monopolists. Recently, General Electric, usually cited as a well-managed monopoly, but which had previously been convicted of major criminal antitrust violations, pleaded guilty to defrauding the Air Force by forging worker's time cards on a Minuteman missile contract. General Dynamics has admitted to $75 million in defense overcharges. Currently, over half of the nation's largest defense contractors, those who the Department of Defense favors with sole source contracts, are under criminal investigation for fraud.

Our Department of Defense has fallen into the very same trap as the French Government, in thinking that the giant monopolies operate more efficiently than small enterprises. In truth, a small enterprise is far more motivated toward efficiency, because each segment of its business means so much to it. For the owners and managers of the monopolies the proper execution of business affairs is becoming an abstraction in search of ever increasing sales and profits.

Thus, in an effort to rid our national defense of the predatory monopolies, **Metacapitalism's** budget cuts defense spending for 1986 from the Administration's proposed $285.7 billion to $215 billion, which is five percent of GNP. Except in times of war, given nuclear parity in destructive capability, defensive systems, and delivery systems, the spending of more than five percent of GNP for national defense is socially and economically unbalanced.

International Affairs

Government spending allocated to international affairs aims to promote a peaceful world environment, built on international security and prosperity, in which individuals may enjoy political and economic freedom. Given current world volatility, particularly in the Middle East, South and Central America, and the continuing famines in Africa and India, the Administration's proposed $18.3 billion simply does not face up to world realities. In order to help thwart hunger and geopolitical communism wherever it appears, **Metacapitalism's** budget more than doubles funds allocated to international affairs to $43 billion.

General Science, Space, and Technology

Advanced industrial societies require significant investments in pure research, at levels and about matters inappropriate for individual businesses. America verges on significant breakthroughs in all areas of science, particularly in food growth, fatal diseases, and the protection of our citizenry from nuclear attack. The puny $9.3 billion ear-marked by the Administration is grossly imprudent. *Metacapitalism's* budget proposes a minimum permanent allocation to research of .5 percent of GNP, which ups the budget in 1986 from $9.3 billion to $21.5 billion.

Natural Resources and the Environment

Funds allocated to this function are primarily for the improvement of water resources, conservation and land management, recreational resources, and pollution control. The Administration has cut this budget from a peak in 1980 of $13.9 billion to $10.8 billion in 1986. At bottom, these cuts show an utter disregard for the well-being of the nation's present population and the generations yet to come. A pure and accessible water supply, clean air, clean earth, and the preservation and cultivation of public lands for recreational use are high on the list of measures of a nation's quality of life. Toxic material is not dumped in the backyards of the wealthy. Public land does not suit their elitist recreational pursuits. Thus, the Administration, tilted as it is in favor of the wealthy, has seen fit to cut these funds drastically. *Metacapitalism's* budget allocates a minimum of .5 percent of GNP to the natural resource and environmental function, which comes to $21.5 billion in 1986.

Agriculture

Administration policies seem intent on destroying the concept of the family farm. Of course, as with every matter of economic import, they say one thing, and then do precisely the opposite. Administration cuts in farm income stabilization, down from $21.3 billion in 1983 to $6.6 billion in 1986, have all but decimated small farms. Free market prices for farm products is a desirable objective, but alternatives exist for achieving this objective without forcing the nation's entire small farming community into the lines of the unemployed.

Metacapitalism proposes an agricultural budgetary allotment of .5 percent of GNP, supplemented by significant funding from the National Capital Act. The lion's share of these funds would be directed toward the rescue of the small farming families and the establishment of new small farms. The Administration has proposed a total of $12.6 billion for agriculture in 1986. *Metacapitalism's* budget allocates .5 percent of GNP, or $21.5 billion, plus a

significant share of the $107.5 billion that is raised by the
National Capital Act to provide capitalization for small
businesses and farms.

Transportation

In 1949 the General Motors Corporation was convicted of conspiracy to destroy the nation's mass transit
systems, and fined $5,000. The fine was so low, perhaps
because mass-transit in America was already in a sham-
bles. Our nation has seriously neglected its transportation. In the cities, such mass-transit as may be found is
usually in a state of advanced decay. The commuting system from the nation's suburbs, is full of waste and inefficiency. Many people are forced to spend more than
one-eighth of their waking hours in the commute to and
from work. **Metacapitalism's** budget would allocate one
percent of GNP to transportation, or $43 billion as com-
pared to the Administration's $25.9 billion.

Community and Regional Development

It is pure delusion that this function occupies a line
in the Administration's budget. The Administration has
allocated $7.3 billion in 1986, an amount barely sufficient
to keep this vital function alive. **Metacapitalism's** Com-

munity Participation Act envisions a permanent funding of 2.5 percent of GNP, or $107.5 billion in 1986. That act defines the specific uses to which the funds would be put, all of which serve to improve the quality of life for all Americans.

Education, Training, Employment, and the Social Services

The administration has reduced the funding for this function from $33.7 billion in 1981 to $29.3 billion in 1986, reflecting its policy of abandoning the educationally disadvantaged, low-income, and handicapped persons. The administration also shows marked disdain for the millions of middle income families who can no longer afford a higher education for their children. Higher education in America was once the exclusive province of the wealthy and this administration's educational funding policies appear to favor a return to those days, just one of any number of its insidiously retrogressive policies. By its National Education Act, **Metacapitalism** proposes that a permanent seven percent of GNP be allocated to this all-important function, or $301 billion, $125 billion of which would represent a transfer of state and local property taxes to the federal government, and another $125 billion of which would be direct loans to students to fund higher education and vocational training. Thus, actual spending over the administration's projections is only $21.7 billion.

Health

Under this function, the Administration lists only those funds allocated to Medicaid, $23.7 billion, health research, $5.2 billion, and consumer protection, $1.1 billion, with $5.9 billion unaccounted for. To get a truer picture of funds allocated to health, we should calculate Medicare at $67 billion, and hospital and medical care for veterans at $10 billion, to give a total of $112.9 billion. But this is only the tip of the iceberg. Tax subsidies in the form of corporate and individual income tax deductions add at least $100 million to this figure. In fact, the nation's health bill, both public and private is rapidly approaching eleven percent of GNP, for an annual total of $473 billion. **Metacapitalism's** National Medical Care Act proposes sweeping changes to the funding and direction of the nation's health care establishment. Monopolistic forces within the medical industry have driven medical costs beyond all sense. **Metacapitalism's** budget for health is seven percent of GNP, or $301 billion, and provides for equitable health care for all Americans.

Income Security

The administration has divided Income Security into two functional line items (1) Social Security and Medicare, which account for $202 billion, and $67.4 billion, respectively. (2) Income Security, which, in total, is $115.8 billion, and reflects $47.1 billion for various categories of federal employees, railroad employees, coal miners, the military, and dependents and survivors. The sum total of the two Administration functional line items is $385.2 billion, less the $100 plus billion for health, leaves $265.9 billion, a figure quite insufficient to provide income security to a nation nearing a population of 250 million.

With its Income Security Act, aided by its Prosperity Revenue Act, **Metacapitalism** has proposed the National Productivity Dividend which will replace most income security programs. The Productivity Dividend would be set at an annual level of approximately twenty-five percent of GNP, about half of which would be raised by corporate and individual income taxes, and the other half by a tax on corporate and individual wealth. The projected sum for 1986 is $1.075 trillion.

Net Interest

The Administration projects net interest payments in 1986 of $142.6 billion, which, given their propensity for running up the deficit, will be far too low if interest rates remain at their present levels. As we have seen in the Financial Reform Act, these interest payments are an unseen tax increase for low and middle income groups and serve mainly to enhance the financial positions of the wealthy. **Metacapitalism** proposes that a fair and equitable monetarization of the federal debt be implemented. Since it is entrenched wealth that has been the primary beneficiary of the accumulated federal debt, it is only fair that it should bear the burden of its monetarization.

Other Functional Items

Into this catchall function falls Energy, Commerce and Housing Credit, General Government, and General Purpose and Fiscal Assistance. The administration proposes $21.1 billion. *Metacapitalism* proposes raising this to $43.0 billion, primarily for an enhanced administration of justice, as set forth in the Judicial Reform Act.

National Capital Fund

The administration has proposed elimination of even the meager funds now allocated to the Small Business Administration. In the past, SBA had provided less than one billion dollars annually to small enterprises, by way of interest bearing loans. *Metacapitalism* proposes an intensive acceleration of capital to small enterprises, businesses and farms, by allocating 2.5 percent of GNP, or $107.5 billion in 1986, in non-interest loans.

Comparative Budget Conclusions

Budgets represent far more than mere anticipations of future spending levels. Budgets are the monetary quan-

tification of ideologies, be they business or government.
Businesses that budget heavily for research and development usually intend to create and market new products.
Thus, it may be said that they postulate their future
growth at least in part on new product development.
Businesses that do not provide funding for research and
development may grow either by intensifying the market-
ing of existing product lines or by acquiring other businesses. Generally speaking, businesses that do not grow
tend to stagnate and then deteriorate. The same is true of
people and governments.

The administration's budget, though in heavy deficit,
is a budget of stagnation in every vital function of our
government except defense, and even in this area much of
the spending is wasteful. The only item in the administration's budget that has worked to ward off economic chaos
since 1982 is the deficit, which if we can believe them, is
an accident, since they have repeatedly declared that they
much prefer a balanced budget. Their budget reflects their
Darwinian economic perspective, that only the fittest shall
survive the rigors of the marketplace. But, as we have
seen, for this administration, fit means wealthy. They see
the wealthy as entitled to every possible governmental
protection, from an unconscionable array of tax preferences, subsidies, and shelters to huge government bailouts of thrashing corporate giants, to encouraging
corporate criminality by choosing not to enforce the
nation's antitrust laws, pandering to special business
interests and encouraging an environment of corrupt
business practices. The administration's budget is the

quantitative manifestation of the wedding of the federal government and the economic monopolists, a perfectly virulent form of socialism. As presently constituted, their budget seeks the continuance of economic insecurity for the vast majority of Americans. It seeks the further monopolization of the farming industry by the financial manipulations of the economic monopolists. It seeks the further deterioration of our nation's mass transit systems. It seeks to continue the hidden tax upon the low and middle income groups by spending more than fifteen percent of federal funds on interest payments to the wealthy, by far the fastest growing segment of the administration's budget, eclipsing even national defense. Communities and the poor are all but ignored, as are retirees who can look forward to even greater income deterioration as the administration continues its attack on Social Security. All told, every aspect of the administration's budget is very troubling. Along with the poor and the elderly, aid to troubled nations and funds for domestic research and development are all but ignored. And perhaps worst of all for the future of our nation is the administration's hostility toward education. The administration, as reflected in its budget and its words and deeds, seeks a return to the days when only the wealthy could afford a university education, a truly repugnant notion by even the least democratic standards. Finally, the administration's budget encapsulates the full retrogressive evil of government by unworthy amateurs in the interests of the few, the economic monopolists, and against the vast majority of Americans that it wishes to continue in economic slavery.

Metacapitalism's budget is designed to fully support each of its legislative initiatives, which are themselves intended to stimulate the evolution of capitalism and democracy from the stagnancy and uncertainty that has beset them. Function by function, *Metacapitalism's* budget is consistent with increasing real freedom for all Americans, by promoting the general interests of all Americans over special interest considerations. Whenever a special interest appears, except for the neediest among us, it is stripped away. The economic role of government with *Metacapitalism* is greatly increased, while its intrusive role is greatly reduced.

LIFE IN AMERICA
WITH *METACAPITALISM*

Many themes have been synthesized to create **Meta-capitalism.** Among the more important of those discussed are an increased awareness of the complexity of the historic struggle now occurring between American capitalism and Soviet communism, particularly the competition for economic superiority. The Soviets seek to demonstrate that state control of a nation's productive apparatus yields a better life for a nation's citizenry than private ownership. This argument is centerpiece of their justification of communism and its inherent limitations on human freedom, not to mention its virtual enslavement of hundreds of millions of Soviet citizens towards this end.

We have seen that American capitalism and American democracy have reached a great plateau, a level from which we must necessarily advance or retreat. The forces of the status quo are content to retreat. Their lives seem to them as fulfilled as possible and they are blind to the long-range implications of their retrogressive inhumane, and naive policy formulations. They regularly wrap themselves in our Constitution as if to do so assures their patriotism.

True patriots seek to make our Constitution live by continuously striving to modernize it, to make it reflect the social, economic, and political interests of all Americans. False patriots, the stalwart guardians of the status quo, seek only to use the Constitution as a means for repressing the evolution of democracy and the spread of economic security to all Americans. They seek the continuous elevation of property rights over human rights and in doing so disgrace us all.

With **Metacapitalism's** proposed legislative initiatives life in America will be greatly changed. Economic development will be enormously accelerated by the Prosperity Revenue, Economic Planning, and National Capital Acts. Economic security and the quality of life will be vastly improved by the Income Security Act's National Productivity Dividend, the National Medical Care Act, and the Judicial Reform Act. Government will be streamlined, the special interests and economic monopolies routed, and true democracy initiated by the Political Reform Act, the Financial Reform Act, and the Judicial Reform Act. Citizen alienation will be greatly reduced by the directed democracy inherent in the Voting Powers Act and the widespread community action facilitated by the Community Participation Act. The harsh consequences of economic recessions will be mitigated by the Income Security and Economic Planning Acts, and the Corporate and Financial Reform Acts will work to thwart the reoccurrence of an economic depression as was experienced in the 1930s. By redirecting our economy from concentrated economic power to decentralized economic power with an economic policy that favors small enterprise over monopolies, the productivity of American capitalism will surge. And, the human resources so necessary for this resurgence will be given great impetus by the National Education, the Community Participation, and the National Capital Acts. In sum, *Metacapitalism* will use and expand upon the productive powers that emanate from a free society (democracy is capitalism's greatest strength) to fashion a better life for all Americans and to negate the Soviet economic challenge.

Metacapitalism has shown how both capitalism and democracy may continue to evolve; capitalism in the main by ridding itself of the economic monopolists and chimerical economic theories; democracy by streamlining the processes of government and moving from representational (illusory) democracy to direct (true) democracy. Societies and economic laws are fashioned by men and women and should not be considered as immutable or natural. What has been created by people may be revitalized, re-created by people. On this planet, and perhaps throughout the universe, there is nothing more important than "The People, Yes."

BIBLIOGRAPHY

Aaron, Henry J. *Economic Effects of Social Security.* Washington, D.C.: The Brookings Institution, 1982.

Acheson, Patricia C. *Our Federal Government, How it Works: An Introduction to the United States Government, 4th ed.* New York: Dodd, Mead & Co., 1984.

Ackerman, Bruce A. *Social Justice in the Liberal State.* New Haven and London: Yale University Press, 1980.

Ader, Emile B. *Communism: Classic and Contemporary.* Woodbury: Barron's Educational Series, Inc., 1970.

Adler, Mortimer J. *A Vision of the Future: Twelve Ideas for a Better Life and a Better Society.* New York and London: Macmillan Co., 1984.

Alcaly, Roger E., and Mermelstein, David. *The Fiscal Crisis of American Cities.* New York: Vintage Books, a division of Random House, 1977.

Angell, Norman. *Why Freedom Matters.* New York: Penguin Books, 1940.

Arendt, Hannah. *Between Past and Future: Eight Exercises in Political Thought.* New York: Viking Press, 1968.

Arendt, Hannah. *The Human Condition.* Chicago and London: The University of Chicago Press, 1970.

BIBLIOGRAPHY

Backman, Jules, ed. *Business and the American Economy: 1776-2001*. With an introduction by Harold S. Geneen. New York: New York University Press, 1976.

Bailyn, Bernard. *The Ideological Origins of the American Revolution*. Cambridge: The Belknap Press of Harvard University Press, 1967.

Barber, Benjamin R. *Strong Democracy: Participatory Politics for a New Age*. Berkeley, Los Angeles, and London: University of California Press, 1984.

Barney, Gerald O. *The Global 2000 Report to the President: Entering the Twenty-First Century*, Vol 1. Washington, D.C.: U.S. Government Printing Office, 1977.

Beckman, Robert C. *The Downwave: Surviving the Second Great Depression*. New York: E.P. Dutton Inc., 1983.

Beer, Samuel H., ed. *Marx and Engels: The Communist Manifesto*. Northbrook: AHM Publishing Corp., 1955.

Bell, Daniel, and Kristol, Irving, ed. *The Crisis in Economic Theory*. New York: Basic Books, Inc., 1981.

Benne, Robert. *The Ethic of Democratic Capitalism: A Moral Reassessment*. Philadelphia: Fortress Press, 1981.

Bernstein, Peter L. *The Price of Prosperity: A Realistic Appraisal of the Future of our National Economy*. New York: Vintage Books, a division of Random House, 1966.

Bolling, Richard, and Bowles, John. *America's Competitive Edge: How to Get Our Country Moving Again*. New York: McGraw-Hill Book Co., 1982.

Boorstin, Daniel J. *Democracy and its Discontents: Reflections on Everyday America*. New York: Vintage Books, a division of Random House, 1975.

Boorstin, Daniel J. *The Americans: The Democratic Experience*. New York: Vintage Books, a division of Random House, 1974.

288

BIBLIOGRAPHY

Boskin, Michael J., ed. *The Economy in the 1980's: A Program For Growth and Stability.* San Francisco: Institute for Contemporary Studies, 1980.

Boskin, Michael J., ed. *Federal Tax Reform: Myths and Realities.* San Francisco: Institute for Contemporary Studies, 1978.

Bradley, Bill. *The Fair Tax.* New York: Simon & Shuster, Inc., 1984.

Brown, Bernard E. *Great American Political Thinkers,* Vol. I. New York: Avon Books, 1983.

Burns, Arthur F. *Reflections of an Economic Policy Maker: Speeches and Congressional Statements, 1969-1978.* Washington, D.C.: American Enterprise Institute for Public Policy Research, 1978.

Burns, James MacGregor. *Leadership.* New York: Harper Colophon Books, Harper B Row, Publishers, 1979.

Califano, Joseph A., Jr. *Governing America.* New York: Simon and Schuster, 1981.

Carnoy, Martin, and Shearer, Derek. *Economic Democracy: The challenge of the 1980's.* Armonk: M. E. Sharpe, Inc. 1980.

Carnoy, Martin; Shearer, Derek; and Rumberger, Russell. *A New Social Contract: The Economy and Government After Reagan.* New York: Harper & Row, 1983.

Carroll, Peter N., and Noble, David W. *The Free and the Unfree: A New History of the United States.* New York: Penguin Books, 1977.

Church, Joseph. *America the Possible: Why and How the Constitution Should be Rewritten.* New York: Macmillan Publishing Co., 1982.

Clower, Robert W., ed. *Articles and Shorter Papers.* New York: The American Economic Review, March 1983.

Clower, Robert W., ed. *Articles and Shorter Papers.* New York: The American Economic Review, December 1983.

Cohen, Stephen S. *Modern Capitalist Planning: The French Model*. Berkeley, Los Angeles, and London: University of California Press, 1977.

Committee for Economic Development. *Productivity Policy: Key to the Nation's Economic Future*. New York, 1983.

The Conference Board. *Challenge to Leadership: Managing In a Changing World*. New York: The Free Press, a division of Macmillan Publishing Co., Inc. 1973.

Cooke, Edward F. *A Detailed Analysis of the Constitution*. Torowa: Rowman & Allanheld, 1984.

Cornuelle, Richard. *Healing America: What can be Done About the Continuing Economic Crisis*. New York: G. P. Putnam's Sons, 1983.

Council of Economic Advisors. *Economic Report of the President*. Washington, D.C.: U.S. Government Printing Office, 1985.

Davidson, James Dale. *The Squeeze*. New York: Summit Books, a division of Simon & Schuster, 1980.

Debray, Régis. *Revolution in the Revolution?: Armed Struggle and Political Struggle in Latin America*. Translated by Bobbye Ortiz. New York: Grove Press, Inc., 1967.

Degler, Carl N. *The Age of the Economic Revolution: 1876-1900*. Glenview: Scott, Foresman and Co.,

Dewey, John. *Individualism: Old and New*. New York: Capricorn Books Edition, 1962.

Directorate of Intelligence, C.I.A. *Handbook of Economic Statistics, 1984*. Washington, D.C.: U.S. Government Printing Office, 1984.

Diven, Frances Fox, and Cloward, Richard A. *The New Class War: Reagan's Attack on the Welfare State and It's Consequences*. New York: Pantheon Books, a division of Random House, 1982.

BIBLIOGRAPHY

Dobb, Maurice. *Studies in the Development of Capitalism.* New York: International Publishers, 1981.

Dorsen, Norman, ed. *Our Endangered Rights: The ACLU Report on Civil Liberties Today.* New York and Toronto: Random House, 1984.

Dowd, Douglas F. *The Twisted Dream: Capitalist Development in the United States Since 1776.* Cambridge: Winthrop Publishers, Inc., 1974.

Duffy, James H. *Domestic Affairs: American Programs and Priorities.* New York: Simon and Schuster, 1978.

Durkheim, Emile. *The Division of Labor Society.* Translated by George Simpson. New York: The Free Press, 1964.

Ehrlich, Paul R. *The End of Affluence.* New York: Ballantine Books, a division of Random House, 1980.

Eisenstadt, S. N., ed., with an introduction. *Max Weber: On Charisma and Institution Building.* Chicago and London: The University of Chicago Press, 1968.

Engels, Frederick. *Socialism: Utopian and Scientific.* Peking: Foreign Languages Press, 1975.

Etzioni, Amitai. *Capital Corruption: The New Attack on American Democracy.* San Diego, New York, and London: Harcourt Brace Jovanovich, 1984.

Executive Office of the President: Office of Management and Budget. *Budget of the United States Government, Fy 1985.* Washington, D.C.: U.S. Government Printing Office, 1985.

Executive Office of the President: Office of Management and Budget. *Handbook of Economic Statistics, 1984.* Washington, D.C.: U.S. Government Printing Office, September 1984.

Executive Office of the President: Office of Management and Budget. *Major Themes and Additional Budget Details, Fy 1985.* Washington, D.C.: Government Printing Office.

BIBLIOGRAPHY

Executive Office of the President: Office of Management and Budget. *Special Analyses: Budget of the United States Government, Fy 1985.* Washington, D.C.: U.S. Government Printing Office, 1985.

Executive Office of the President: Office of Management and Budget. *The United States Budget in Brief, Fy 1986.* Washington, D.C.: Government Printing Office, 1985.

Forman, James D. *Communism: From Marx's Manifesto to 20th-Century Reality.* New York: Dell Publishing Co., Inc., 1972.

Foucault, Michel. *Madness and Civilization: A History of Insanity in the Age of Reason.* New York, Toronto, and London: New American Library, Inc., 1971.

Frankel, Marvin E. *Criminal Sentences: Law Without Order.* New York: Hill and Wang, a division of Farrar, Straus, and Groux, 1973.

Freedman, Robert, ed. *Marx on Economics.* With an Introduction by Harry Schwartz. New York: Harcourt, Brace and Co., 1961.

Freeman, Roger A. *A Preview and Summary of the Wayward Welfare State.* Stanford: Hoover Institution Press, 1981.

Friedman, Milton, and Friedman, Rose. *Free to Choose: A Personal Statement.* New York: Avon Books, 1981.

Friedman, Milton, and Friedman, Rose. *Tyranny of the Status Quo.* San Diego, New York, and London: Harcourt Brace Jovanovich, 1984.

Galbraith, John Kenneth. *The Affluent Society,* 3rd edition. New York and Scarborough, ON, 1976.

Galbraith, John Kenneth. *Economics & the Public Purpose.* New York: New American Library, 1973.

Galbraith, John Kenneth. *The Liberal Hour.* New York: New American Library, 1960.

Galbraith, John Kenneth. *The New Industrial State*. New York: New American Library, 1978.

Gallup, George, Comp. *America Wants to Know: The Issues & the Answers of the Eighties*. New York: A & W Publishers, Inc., 1983.

Gilbert, Neil. *Capitalism and the Welfare State: Dilemmas of Social Benevolence*. New Haven and London: Yale University Press, 1983.

Gilder, George. *Wealth and Poverty*. New York: Bantom Books, Inc., 1981.

Glock, Charles Y., and Hammond, Phillip E. *Beyond the Classics?: Essays in the Scientific Study of Religion*. New York: Harper & Row, Publishers, 1973.

Goldston, Robert. *The Great Depression: The United States in the Thirties*. New York: Fawcett Premier Books, 1968.

Goldston, Robert. *The Russian Revolution*. New York: Fawcett Premier Books, 1966.

Goodin, Robert E. *Political Theory & Public Policy*. Chicago and London: University of Chicago Press, 1982.

Greene, Leonard M. *Free Enterprise Without Poverty*. New York and London: W. W. Norton & Co., 1983.

Haldeman, H. R. with DiMona, Joseph. *The Ends of Power*. New York: Dell Publishing Co., Inc., 1978.

Hall, Robert E., and Rabushka, Alvin. *Low Tax, Simple Tax, Flat Tax*. New York: McGraw-Hill Book Co., 1983.

Harrington, Michael. *The Other America: Poverty in the United States*. New York: Penguin Books, 1981.

Hart, Gary. *A New Democracy: A Democratic Vision for the 1980's and Beyond*. New York: William Morrow and Co. Inc., 1983.

BIBLIOGRAPHY

Hawken, Paul. *The Next Economy.* New York: Holt, Rinehart and Winston, 1983.

Hayden, Tom. *The American Future: New Visions Beyond the Reagan Administration.* New York: Washington Square Press, a division of Simon and Schuster, 1982.

Heckscher, Gunnar. *The Welfare State and Beyond: Success and Problems in Scandinavia.* Minneapolis: University of Minnesota Press, 1984.

Heilbroner, Robert L. *An Inquiry into the Human Prospect.* New York and London: W. W. Norton & Company, Inc., 1980.

Heilbroner, Robert L. *Between Capitalism and Socialism: Essays in Political Economics.* New York: Vintage Books, a division of Random House, 1970.

Heilbroner, Robert L. *Business Civilization in Decline.* New York: W. W. Norton & Company, Inc., 1976.

Heilbroner, Robert L. *The Limits of American Capitalism.* New York: Harper & Row, 1967.

Heilbroner, Robert L. *The Making of Economic Society.* Englewood Cliffs: Prentice-Hall, Inc., 1964.

Heilbroner, Robert L. *The Worldly Philosophers: The Lives, Times, and Ideas of the Great Economic Thinkers.* New York: Simon and Schuster, 1980.

Hobsbawm, E. J. *The Age of Revolution: 1789-1848.* New York: New American Library, 1962.

Hook, Sidney. *Marx and the Marxists: The Ambiguous Legacy.* Princeton: D. Van Nostrand Co., Inc., 1955.

Hughes, H. Stuart. *Consciousness and Society: The Reorientation of European Social Thought 1890-1930.* New York: Vintage Books, a division of Random House, 1961.

BIBLIOGRAPHY

Hutchings, Raymond. *Soviet Economic Development,* 2nd ed. New York and London: New York University Press, 1982.

The International Bank. *World Development Report 1984.* New York: Oxford University Press, 1984.

Joint Economic Committee Congress of the United States. *February 1984: Economic Report of the President.* Washington, D.C.: U.S. Government Printing Office, 1984.

Kaiser, Robert G. *Russia: The People and the Power.* New York: Simon and Schuster, 1976.

Kant, Immanuel. *Critique of Pure Reason.* Translated by Norman Kemp Smith. New York: St. Martin's Press, 1929.

Kant, Immanuel. *Foundations of the Metaphysics of Morals.* Indianapolis and New York: The Bobbs-Merrill Co., Inc., 1959.

Koyré, Alexandre. *From the Closed World: To the Infinite Universe.* Baltimore and London: The Johns Hopkins Press, 1957.

Kristol, Irving. *Two Cheers for Capitalism.* New York: New American Library, 1979.

Lamprecht, Sterling P., ed. *Locke: Selections.* New York: Charles Scribner's Sons, 1956.

Lebergott, Stanley. *The American Economy: Income, Wealth, and Want.* Princeton: Princeton University Press, 1976.

Lekachman, Robert. *Greed is Not Enough: Reaganomics.* New York: Random House Inc., 1982.

Lekachman, Robert. *A History of Economic Ideas.* New York: McGraw-Hill, 1976.

Lévi-Strauss, Claude. *Tristes Tropiques.* Translated by John and Doreen Weightman. New York: Atheneum, 1973.

Lijphart, Arend. *Democracies: Patterns of Majoritarian and Consensus Government in Twenty-One Countries.* New Haven and London: Yale University Press, 1984.

Lodge, George C. *The American Disease.* New York: Alfred A. Knopf, Inc., 1984.

Lowith, Karl. *Meaning in History.* Chicago and London: University of Chicago Press, 1970.

Lykova, L. *Social Security.* Moscow: Novosti Press Agency Publishing House, 1970.

Maisel, F. W. *The Great American Ripoff.* San Diego: Condido Press, 1983.

Mandelbaum, Maurice. *The Problem of Historical Knowledge: An Answer to Relativism.* New York, Evanston, and Cordon: Harper & Row, Publishers, 1967.

Mannheim, Karl. *Ideology and Utopia: An introduction to the Sociology of Knowledge.* Translated by Louis Wirth and Edward Shils. New York: Harcourt, Brace & World, Inc., 1936.

Marx, Karl. *The Poverty of Philosophy.* Peking: Foreign Languages Press, 1978.

Marx, Karl. *Wages, Price and Profit.* Peking: Foreign Languages Press, 1975.

Marx, Karl, and Engels, Frederick. *The Communist Manifesto.* With an introduction by A. J. P. Taylor. New York: Penguin Books, 1978.

Marx, Karl, and Engels, Frederick. *Manifesto of the Communist Party.* Peking: Foreign Languages Press, 1972.

Marx, Karl, and Engels, Frederick. *Selected Letters.* Peking: Foreign Languages Press, 1977.

Mathews, R. C. O., and Sargent, J. R. *Contemporary Problems of Economic Policy: Essays from the CLARE Group.* New York and London: Methuen & Co., 1983.

McNamara, Robert S. *The Essence of Security: Reflections in Office.* New York, Evanston, and London: Harper & Row, Publishers, 1968.

Meade, James E. *The Intelligent Radicals Guide to Economic Policy: The Mixed Economy.* London: George Allen & Unwin Ltd., 1980.

Mendel, Arthur P., ed. *Essential Works of Marxism.* New York: Bantam Books, 1965.

Merritt, Richard L. *Systematic Approaches to Comparative Politics.* Chicago: Rand McNally & Co., 1971.

Miles, Marc A. *Beyond Monetarism: Finding the Road to Stable Money.* New York: Basic Books, Inc., 1984.

Miller, S. M., and Tomaskovic-Devey, Donald. *Recapitalizing America: Alternatives to the Corporate Distortion of National Policy.* Boston: Routledge & Kegan Paul, 1983.

Miller, William, ed. *Regrowing: The American Economy.* Englewood Cliffs: Prentice-Hall, Inc., 1983.

Morgenbesser, Sidney, and Walsh, James, ed. *Free Will.* Englewood Cliffs: Prentice-Hall Inc., 1962.

Mrachkovskaya, I. M. *From Revisionism to Betrayal: A Criticism of OTA Sik's Economic Views.* Moscow: Progress Publishers, 1972.

Murchland, Bernard. *Humanism and Capitalism: A Survey of Thought on Morality.* Washington, D.C. and London: American Enterprise Institute for Public Policy Research, 1984.

Nathan, Richard P.; Cook, Robert F.; and Rawlins, V. Lane. *Public Service Employment: A Field Evaluation.* Washington, D.C.: The Brookings Institution, 1981.

National Tax Limitation Committee. *Meeting America's Economic Crisis: A "Road Map" To Emergency Federal Spending Reductions.* Foreword by David Stockman. Washington, D.C.: Caroline House Publishers, Inc., 1981.

Nelson, Benjamin. *The Idea of Usury: From Tribal Brotherhood to Universal Otherhood.* Chicago and London: The University of Chicago Press, 1969.

Netzer, Dick. *Economics of the Property Tax.* Washington, D.C.: The Brookings Institution, 1970.

Nevins, Allan, and Commager, Henry Steele. *A Pocket History of the United States,* 7th ed. New York: Pocket Books, a division of Simon & Schuster, 1981.

Nikitin, P. I. *The Fundamentals of Political Economy.* Moscow: Progress Publishers, 1983.

Nisbet, Robert A. *The Quest for Community.* London, Oxford, and New York: Oxford University Press, 1981.

North, Douglass C. *Growth and Welfare In the American Past: A New Economic History.* Englewood Cliffs: Prentice-Hall, Inc., 1966.

Norwick, Kenneth P. ed. *Lobbying for Freedom in the 1980's: A Grass-Roots Guide to Protecting Your Rights.* New York: G. P. Putnam's Sons, 1983.

Novak, Michael. *The Spirit of Democratic Capitalism.* New York: Simon and Schuster, 1983.

Nozick, Robert. *Philosophical Explanations.* Cambridge: The Belknap Press of Harvard University Press, 1983.

Olafson, Frederick A., ed. *Justice and Social Policy: A Collection of Essays.* Englewood Cliffs: Prentice-Hall, Inc., 1961.

Olson, Mancur. *The Rise and Decline of Nations: Economic Growth, Stagflation, and Social Rigidities.* New Haven and London: Yale University Press, 1982.

Paarlberg, Don. *Great Myths of Economics*. New York and Scarborough, ON: New American Library, Inc., 1971.

Page, Benjamin I. *Who Gets What From Government*. Berkley, Los Angeles, and London: University of California Press, 1983.

Paine, Thomas. *Rights of Man*. With a biographical introduction by Philip S. Foner. Secaucus: Citadel Press Inc., 1974.

Pauly, Mark V. *National Health Insurance: What Now, What Later, What Never?* Washington, D.C.: American Enterprise Institute for Public Policy Research, 1980.

Payer, Cheryl. *The World Bank: A Critical Analysis*. New York and London: Monthly Review Press, 1982.

Pechman, Joseph A., ed. *Setting National Priorities: Agenda for the 1980's*. Washington, D.C.: The Brookings Institution, 1980.

Pirenne, Henri. *Economic and Social History of Medieval Europe*. New York and London: Harcourt Brace Jovanovich, 1937.

Piven, Frances Fox, and Cloward, Richard A. *The New Class War: Reagan's Attack on the Welfare State and Its Consequences*. New York: Pantheon Books, 1982.

Piven, Frances Fox, and Cloward, Richard A. *Regulating the Poor: The Functions of Public Welfare*. New York: Vintage Books, a division of Random House, 1971.

Polenberg, Richard, ed. *America at War: The Home Front 1941-1945*. Englewood Cliffs: Prentice-Hall, Inc., 1968.

President's Commission for a National Agenda for the Eighties. *Government and the Regulation of Corporate and Individual Decisions in the Eighties*. Washington, D.C.: U.S. Government Printing Office, 1980.

President's Commission for a National Agenda for the Eighties. *The United States and the World Community in the Eighties*. Washington, D.C.: U.S. Government Printing Office, 1980.

299

Revel, Jean-Francois. *How Democracies Perish.* Translated by William Byron. New York: Doubleday & Co., Inc., 1983.

Riley, John G., and St. John, Wilma. *The American Economic Review: Papers and Proceedings of the Ninety-Fifth Annual Meeting.* New York: American Economic Association, May 1983.

Ringer, Robert J. *Restoring the American Dream.* New York: Fawcett Crest, 1980.

Rohatyn, Felix G. *The Twenty-Year Century: Essays on Economics and Public Finance.* New York: Random House, Inc., 1983.

Rotwein, Eugene, ed., with an introduction. *David Hume: Writings on Economics.* Madison: University of Wisconsin Press, 1970.

Ruff, Howard J. *Survive and Win in the Inflationary Eighties.* With a foreword by Senator Orrin Hatch. New York: Warner Books Edition, 1982.

Ryan, William. *Equality.* New York: Vintage Books, a division of Random House, 1982.

Salisbury, Harrison E. *Sakharov Speaks.* New York: Vintage Books, a division of Random House, 1974.

Samuelson, Paul. *Economics: from the Heart.* San Diego, New York, and London: Harcourt Brace Jovanovich, Publishers, 1983.

Santayana, George. *Scepticism and Animal Faith: Introduction to a System of Philosophy.* New York: Dover Publications, Inc., 1955.

Sartre, Jean-Paul. *Search for a Method.* Translated by Hazel E. Barnes. New York: Vintage Books, a Division of Random House, 1963.

Schumpeter, Joseph A. *Business Cycles: A Theoretical, Historical, and Statistical Analysis of the Capitalist Process.* With an introduction by Rendigs Fels. New York, Toronto, and London: McGraw-Hill Book Co., 1964.

Servan-Schreiber, Jean-Jacques. *The Radical Alternative*. With an introduction by John Kenneth Galbraith. New York: W. W. Norton & Co., Inc., 1971.

Shalom, Steve Rosskamm, ed. *Socialist Visions*. Boston: South End Press, 1983.

Shand, Alexander H. *The Capitalist Alternative: An Introduction to Neo-Austrian Economics*. With an introduction by G.L.S. Shackle. New York and London: New York University Press, 1984.

Shipler, David K. *Russia: Broken Idols, Solemn Dreams*. New York: Viking Penguin Inc., 1984.

Shonheld, Andrew. *Modern Capitalism: The Changing Balance of Public and Private Power*. London, Oxford, and New York: Oxford University Press, 1969.

Silk, Leonard. *The Economists*. New York: Avon Books, 1978.

Simon, William E. *A Time for Truth*. New York: Berkley Publishing Corp., 1979.

Sklar, Holly, ed. *Trilateralism: The Trilateral Commission and Elite Planning for World Management*. Boston: South End Press, 1980.

Smith, Adams. *The Wealth of Nations*. With an introduction by Ludwig von Mises. Chicago: Henry Reghery Co., 1953.

Smith, Edward C., ed. *The Constitution of the United States: With Case Summaries*, 10th ed. New York: Barnes & Noble Books, a Division of Harper & Row, Publishers, 1975.

Smith, Jerome F. *The Coming Currency Collapse: and what you can do about it*. New York: Bantom Books, Inc., 1981.

Smith, Michael P. (et al.). *Politics In America: Studies in Policy Analysis*. New York: Random House, 1974.

Starr, Chester G. *The Economic and Social Growth of Early Greece: 800-500 B.C.* New York: Oxford University Press, 1977.

Stein, Herbert. *Presidential Economics: The Making of Economic Policy from Roosevelt to Reagan and Beyond.* New York: Simon and Schuster, 1984.

Sweezy, Paul M. *The Theory of Capitalist Development: Principles of Marxian Political Economy.* New York and London: Modern Reader Paperback, 1968.

Thurow, Lester C. *Dangerous Currents: The State of Economics.* New York: Vintage Books, a division of Random House, 1984.

Thurow, Lester C. *Generating Inequality: Mechanisms of Distribution in the U.S. Economy.* New York: Basic Book, Inc., 1975.

Thurow, Lester C. *The Zero-Sum Society: Distribution and the Possibilities For Economic Change.* New York: Penguin Books, 1982.

Tobias, Andrew. *The Invisible Bankers.* New York: Pocket Books, a division of Simon & Schuster, Inc., 1983.

Tocqueville, Alexis de. *Democracy in America,* Vol II. New York: Vintage Books, a division of Random House, 1945.

Toffler, Alvin. *Previews & Premises.* New York: William Morrow and Co., Inc., 1983.

U.S. Bureau of the Census. *Historical Statistics of the United States: Colonial Times to 1970, Bicentennial Edition, Part 1.* Washington, D.C., 1975.

U.S. Bureau of the Census. *Historical Statistics of the United States: Colonial Times to 1970, Bicentennial Edition, Part 2.* Washington, D.C., 1975.

U.S. Bureau of the Census. *Statistical Abstract of the United States: 1984, 104th ed.* Washington, D.C., 1983.

Veblen, Thorstein. *On the Nature and Uses of Sabotage*. New York: Oriole Editions, 1919.

Veblen, Thorstein. *The Theory of the Leisure Class: An Economic Study of Institutions*. With an introduction by C. Wright Mills. New York and Scarborough, ON: New American Library, 1953.

Versleg, Clarence L., and Hofstadter, Richard. *Great Issues in American History: From Settlement to Revolution, 1584-1776*. New York: Vintage Books, a division of Random House, 1969.

Von Mises, Ludwig. *Economic Policy: Thoughts for Today and Tomorrow*. Chicago: Regnery Gateway, Inc., 1979.

Wanniski, Jude. *The Way The World Works*. New York: Simon and Shuster, 1983.

Weber, Max. *The Protestant Ethic and the Spirit of Capitalism*. Translated by Talcott Parsons, with an introduction by R. H. Tawney. New York: Charles Scribner's Sons, 1958.

Webster, Bryce, and Perry, Robert L. *The Complete Social Security Handbook*. New York: Dodd, Mead & Co., 1983.

Weeks, John. *Capital and Exploitation*. Princeton: Princeton University Press, 1981.

Wildavsky, Aaron, ed. *Beyond Containment: Alternative American Policies Toward the Soviet Union*. San Francisco: Institute for Contemporary Studies, 1983.

William, Eric. *Capitalism and Slavery*. With an Introduction by D. W. Brogan. London: Andre Deutsch Ltd., 1983.

Willis, Garry. *Exploring America: The Federalist*. New York: Penguin Books, 1982.

BIBLIOGRAPHY

Wilson, George W. *Inflation: Causes, Consequences, and Cures.* Bloomington: Indiana University Press, 1982.

Wolin, Sheldon S., ed. *Democracy: A Journal of Political Renewal and Radical Change.* New York: The Common Good Foundation, 1983.

Young, I. Z. *Doubt and Certainty in Science: A Biologist's Reflections on the Brain.* New York: Oxford University Press, 1960.

Zevin, Robert B. *A Greater Good: Potentials for an Intelligent Economy.* Boston: Houghton Mifflin Co., 1983.

Zinn, Howard. *A People's History of the United States.* New York: Harper & Row, Publishers, 1980.

INDEX

INDEX

O

Office of Management and the
Budget, 147
Official unemployment rate, 167
OPEC, 82, 217
Option markets, 249
Oregon, 139

P

Paraprofessionals, 204
Participative citizenry, 5, 25, 108,
114, 136, 250-51
Participative consciousness,
253-54
Patriots, true and false, 284-86
Penalties, tax, 160
Per capita income, 146
Personal income taxes, 147
Physician-patient relationship,
204
Physicians, 200
Physicians and hospitals
re-certification, 203
Planned obsolescence, 121
Planning, 56, 117, 201, 212, 217,
219
Poland, 40, 145
Political action committees
(PACS), 169, 179, 182
Political Reform Act, 132, 177-82,
221, 286
Pollution control, 274
Population of the United States,
76, 114, 174
Poverty and hunger, 13, 97, 131,
163, 171, 222
Poverty line, national, 153
Presidency, restructuring term of,
182

Presidential appointees, 220
Presidential politics, 232
Primogeniture, 36
Prisons, 258
Princeton University, 184
Privileged classes, children of,
184
Productive apparatus, 129
Productivity Dividend, 9, 22, 28,
152, 158, 173-76
Professional lenders, 239
Profits, 145
Progressive income tax, 144
Prohibition, 195
Property confiscation, 160
Property rights, 60, 107, 181
Property taxes, 156, 174, 185,
187, 267, 277
Prosperity Revenue Act, 132,
142-62, 216, 220
Protectionist strategies, 216
Public school education, 156
Public sector,
see Private and public sectors

Q

Quality health care, as
fundamental entitlement, 151
Quality of life, 4, 12, 108, 128,
222

R

Reagan administration, 226-27
Reagan, Ronald, 143, 150
Reagan-Regan, tax proposal, 143,
149
Recreational resources, 274
Reduced expectations, 96
Religious zealotry, 144

312

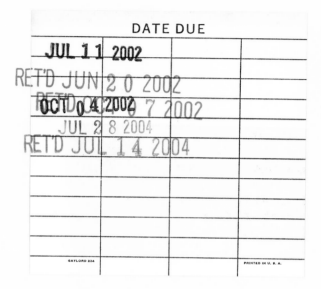